which?
essential guides

DIVO
AND
SPLITTING UP

"Remember, there is life after you have split up. This is your guide to getting there."

Imogen Clout

About the author

Imogen Clout specialised in family law after qualifying as a solicitor and worked at a number of different practices in London. She was an early member of the Solicitors Family Law Association and a founder member of the National Stepfamily Association. She has written on, and taught, family law for many years. Imogen is married with three children.

**which?
essential guides**

DIVORCE
AND
SPLITTING UP

Imogen Clout

Which? Books are commissioned and published by
Which? Ltd, 2 Marylebone Road, London, NW1 4DF
Email: books@which.co.uk

Distributed by Littlehampton Book Services Ltd
Faraday Close, Durrington, Worthing, West Sussex
BN13 3RB

British Library Cataloguing in Publication Data
A catalogue record for this book is available from the British Library

ISBN 978 184490 034 3

Author's a

The author would like to thank Stephen Copeland for his comments on the law
in Northern Ireland and Scott Cochrane and Leonie Burke for the comments on
the law in Scotland.

Editorial/design /production: Luke Block, Angela Newton, Paula Lock at Which?,
Guy Croton, Diarmuid Moloney, Vicky Hales-Dutton and Caroline Watson at
Focus Publishing

Index by: Lynda Swindells

Cover photographs by: Getty Images Ltd
Printed and bound by Scotprint, Scotland

For a full list of Which? Books, please call 01903 828557, access our
website at www.which.co.uk, or write to Littlehampton Book Services.
For other enquiries call 0800 252 100.

Contents

Introduction

When a long term relationship breaks up you can easily feel as though you are lost. This book aims to help you through what can be a difficult time, and will help you prepare and organize yourself for the future.

Family breakdown is a seemingly impossible situation. You cannot see a way through, and every path seems fraught with difficulty. There are too many things to think about and weigh up, too many choices that you are being forced to make. This book is intended to guide you through this difficult process, highlighting the available options and helping you make the right choices for you and your family.

CIVIL PARTNERS

Since the last edition of this book, the Civil Partnership Act 2004 has come into force. In nearly every aspect, civil partnership law is the same as the law governing marriage. More and more couples are cohabiting now, too. This edition reflects these changes in society. It covers married couples, couples who are civil partners and those who have been living together - regardless of whether they are male-female or same-sex couples. Some aspects of family law are the same for all couples and families, but cohabitees still have much less automatic protection than married/cp couples.

The first section of this book provides information that all couples, whatever their legal status, need if they are splitting up. Then there are specific sections for married/cp couples and cohabiting couples, setting out the particular parts of the law that apply to them. In addition, there are significant differences in the law in Scotland and Northern Ireland, and these are described in Chapter 11.

FINANCE

Breaking up a family is an expensive business. It is very difficult to make the money that once supported one family stretch to two. Added to this are legal costs which most people find onerous. One of the aims of this book is to help you keep those costs down. The best way to do this is not, as you might suppose, to avoid using a lawyer, but rather to find a good one who knows what he or she is doing. It's also a good idea for couples to try to be as civilised to each other as you can, making use of mediation or similar strategies to resolve your differences as amicably as possible.

Not only does this keep your costs down, but it could well sow the seeds for a better relationship in the future. This is vitally important if you have children.

Though many of the decisions you face are likely to be short-term, it is always worth considering the longer term and how you would like your life to develop after this crisis is over. And there is life after the break-up, however remote that time may seem now. This book will help you through the difficult task ahead, until you reach a point when you feel that the worst really is behind you.

A NOTE ON THE LANGUAGE

This book covers the legal aspects for all couples who are in the process of splitting up. There are different legal terms for married couples and civil partners, and the terms used for cohabiting couples are different again. The new words that the law has introduced for civil partnerships make some sentences difficult. What, for instance, is the equivalent of 'married'?

We have tried to be consistent throughout the book and at the same time keep it clear and accurate. This is how we use some of the words:

Jargon buster

Spouse A husband or wife in a married male-female couple.

Civil partner A civil partner in a same sex civil partnership.

Partner If used without qualification: this applies both to a civil partner, or a cohabiting partner (in a same-sex or male female couple).

Cohabitant One of a cohabiting couple (both same-sex and male-female)

Ex A former spouse or partner.

CP A civil partner or a civil partnership - depending on context.

Divorce The ending of a marriage or civil partnership. Although the legislation uses the word dissolution for the ending of a cp, divorce is the normal way of talking about it.

Legal costs

Finding the money to pay for legal advice can be a huge problem if you split up. It is all too easy to 'forget' about the question of costs until your family and financial problems are resolved. However, by that time the total build-up of legal expenses can come as an unexpected shock, severely limiting your own, and your ex's, ability to adapt to your future lives apart.

Costs in family proceedings

The issue of costs can create particularly severe problems when one of you is determined to mount an expensive legal campaign against the other. Whenever you use the law to fight over the children, or over maintenance or property, both of you will generally have to instruct solicitors (and perhaps barristers too). As a result, you will have two bills to pay at the end of the case.

When you are caught up in the thick of the process of splitting up, it is easy to forget that the costs of the proceedings are going to come out of the family money. People involved in acrimonious legal battles often talk about fighting for their 'rights', or 'justice', or 'the principle of the thing', forgetting that all this becomes very expensive, and that family law is not designed to deliver abstract redress or compensation.

This does not mean that it is necessary to cave in to a spouse or partner who is demanding too much. A good solicitor (see Chapter 3 on where to get legal help) will be able to negotiate strongly on your behalf and can in most cases work out a reasonable settlement with your ex's solicitor without the added expenses of a full-blown court battle. You may be able to come to a settlement with your spouse/partner either by yourself or with the aid of a

 This could be the most important chapter of the book for you: please do not be tempted to skip it.

mediator, thus saving considerably on legal costs.

HOW SOLICITORS CHARGE

Solicitors charge according to the amount of time they spend on your case. A solicitor will log every single thing that he or she does on your file: answering letters, making telephone calls, seeing you or witnesses, reading papers, going to court (which includes travelling, waiting and the actual hearing, as well as putting papers in order for trial).

Most solicitors charge on an hourly basis. They usually record the time spent on a case in 'units' of five or six minutes each.

Making a short telephone call or

writing a letter will probably not take as long as this, but the practice is to record them as single units each. If any item of work takes longer than a single unit the time recorded will be rounded up to the nearest unit spent. A further figure (generally worked out as a percentage of the bill) may be added as a mark-up for 'care and attention'. This is an extra charge solicitors make if your case has been complex or has had to be dealt with especially quickly.

When you first instruct a solicitor, or are making enquiries about firms of solicitors, you should check the hourly rate of the person who will be acting for you. Make sure you ask whether the figure you are quoted includes VAT. Solicitors' firms generally have staff who have different levels of legal education and/or experience. Naturally, a partner's hourly charge will be more than that of a trainee or a legal executive.

Bills of costs in legal aid cases are constructed on a slightly different basis. Although, in legal aid cases, the time spent on any one piece of work is taken into account, there are usually pre-set hourly rates for some aspects of the work: travelling to court, for

❝❝ The more you spend on lawyers the less you will have left for yourselves. ❞❞

Jargon buster

Assessment Checking of the amount charged in a bill by the court or Legal Services Commission.

Attendances Face to face meetings.

Brief fee The amount paid to a barrister for an appearance in court. This can be increased by a fee for each additional day spent in court – a 'refresher'.

Bundling Putting papers in order for court.

Conference A meeting with your solicitor and barrister.

Counsel A barrister.

Disbursements Payments made on your behalf, for things like expert reports, valuations.

LSC(Legal Services Commission) This body administers the Legal Aid Scheme.

Perusals Reading the papers on the file.

Refresher The additional amount on a brief fee for each day's work by the barrister in court.

Telephone attendances Phone calls.

See Chapter 3 for information about solicitors. See Chapter 4 for a full explanation of what mediation is, how it works and where to find a mediator.

> **"Time is money when you are using a solicitor. Prepare what you need to say before you telephone or go to an appointment"**

Solicitor's fees

A solicitor's hourly charging rate can be anything from £120 upwards (plus VAT) in a firm outside London; in London it may range from £125 to £250 (plus VAT). Hourly rates of £400 (plus VAT) or more may be charged by senior solicitors at some upmarket London firms.

instance, is charged at a lower rate than actually appearing before a judge. Also certain items, such as routine telephone calls, may be charged at flat rates.

HOW BARRISTERS CHARGE

If your solicitor thinks that your case needs the services of a barrister, either for specialist advice or to represent you in court, you will need to pay a further fee for this. Barristers generally charge on the basis of each piece of work they do: a set amount for a conference, or written advice, or an appearance at court.

Your solicitor negotiates the barrister's fee. This can subsequently be reduced by the court (or in legal aid cases, the Legal Services Commission) in a process known as 'assessment'. You should bear in mind that if your case gets to the stage of a hearing in court and a barrister is instructed to appear for you, the 'brief fee' (the fee for the court appearance) will be charged even if the matter is settled by agreement shortly before the hearing and your barrister does not actually have to represent you at the hearing.

PAYING COSTS YOURSELF

If you are paying privately, your solicitor will probably ask you for some money in advance 'on account of costs'. A sum as large as £500 would not be unusual; indeed, £1,000 is probably more realistic. Your solicitor should send you a bill at regular intervals so that you keep abreast of the costs.

Solicitors have clear professional rules about the information that they must give their clients about costs. At the beginning of your relationship you should be given a letter with full information about the way in which costs will be charged and about the firm's complaints procedure. You

 The Law Society is the professional body regulating solicitors in England and Wales. Its website has useful information about the rules under which solicitors operate and about their charges: www.lawsociety.org.uk/choosingandusing.law

Rules of engagement

If you do not pay your solicitor's bill, he or she is entitled to say that he or she will do no further work for you until the costs are settled. He or she can also retain your file of papers as security for payments.

should be given regular (at least every six months) updates on the level of your costs. You should also be told if the firm increases its charge-out hourly rates. If you have been given an estimate of the likely costs, you should be told if this is going to be exceeded.

When you get a bill from your solicitor you can ask for a break down showing all the items that have been charged for. If you feel that the charges are too high, you should discuss the issue with him or her, or with someone more senior in the firm, and you may be able to agree a reduction. If you are dissatisfied with the response you receive, you are entitled to have your bill assessed (see Assessment on page 27). Normally, you should do this within one month of the date on the bill. Your solicitor should remind you about this in a form of standard wording on the bill. He or she can sue you if you do not pay.

CAN YOU AFFORD THE BILL?

You may not be eligible for legal aid but could still find it hard to pay the solicitor's bill.

Some solicitors have arrangements with credit-card companies and will let you pay using credit cards.

If you are certain that at the end of the case you will get a settlement out of which you can afford to pay your costs, you may be able to persuade your bank to lend you the money, or your solicitor may be prepared to enter into an agreement that he or she will be paid out of this money. This is not a 'contingency fee' agreement – your solicitor is not saying that he or she will be paid only if you win, or that you agree to pay a percentage of what you get. You will still be liable for the costs if you do not get what you had expected, but they should be charged according to the solicitor's normal rates, as agreed with you at the beginning of the case. If your solicitor proposes such an agreement to you, you should be given a draft of the terms and you should consult another independent solicitor before you enter into it. You will need to bear in mind the risks involved, and be aware that costs can increase very rapidly sometimes in ways you had not expected.

❝ Many solicitors will be happy to let you pay by a regular monthly standing order, if this will help to spread the cost. ❞

13

Legal aid

You need to consider whether you will be eligible for legal aid (public funding). This does not mean that you will get your solicitor for free (see page 19 regarding the Statutory Charge), but it will help you meet at least some of the costs.

You can check your eligibility for legal aid on the Community Legal Service website. Both your capital and income are taken into account when your eligibility for legal aid is considered. However, capital which is in dispute between you and your spouse/partner is not included in the calculation. So if you are not working and have little or no income of your own, you may qualify for legal aid even if you have quite a lot of capital that you own as a couple. It can put you at an advantage if your spouse/partner has to pay privately for his/her solicitor.

❝ You do not need to take evidence of your ex-partner's income, as this is not counted if you are divorcing or separating. ❞

Legal aid essentials

You may need the following for your first legal aid appointment:
- Your National Insurance number.
- Your most recent wage slips.
- Proof of income support or income-based jobseeker's allowance if you are out of work and claiming benefits.
- Proof of a tax credit (for example working tax credit).
- Evidence of a partner's income if you live together.

Not all firms of solicitors offer legal aid. If you think that you are eligible, you should check whether a firm offers legal aid when you first make an appointment with it.

If the firm that you go to does offer legal aid and you are eligible, you will find that different levels of the funding apply to different stages of the legal process.

Community Legal Service's national helpline is on 0845 345 4 345. www.clsdirect.org.uk and follow links to the eligibility calculator.

FIRST-STAGE LEGAL AID – LEGAL HELP

First-stage legal aid covers a session of initial advice and the work that the solicitor will do in an undefended divorce/dissolution. However, it covers only the divorce/dissolution itself; not the financial side of things or with any dispute over children. For that there are other forms of legal aid.

When you see your solicitor at the first meeting, he or she will work out whether you qualify for Legal Help. He or she will fill in a form with details of your income and capital. Your disposable capital and disposable income must be under certain limits (which are reviewed annually in April). Your solicitor will be able to tell you immediately whether you are eligible for Legal Help and you will be asked to sign the form with your details to confirm that they are true.

If you are eligible for Legal Help, you will pay nothing to the solicitor. At the end of the case, your solicitor will send the bill to the LSC, which will pay him or her. If you need advice on another legal matter (for example, you might have to deal with a building society over debts and possession proceedings), a new Legal Help form can be completed.

 If at the end of the case you get or keep assets, you will have to pay back to the LSC what it has paid to your solicitor. Known as the Statutory Charge, it does not apply to legal aid for mediation.

If you are receiving Legal Help, you will not have to pay the court fees for divorce proceedings, which is a considerable saving.

SECOND-STAGE LEGAL AID

As stated earlier, Legal Help does not help to arrange the financial aspects of your split, or any dispute over children, apart from your solicitor taking initial instructions from you to find out what the position is and opening negotiations.

Unless your financial circumstances are very straightforward, or you have sorted them all out before you see the solicitor, you will probably need some legal advice and help with negotiating a settlement. If the financial problems are more complicated, or you are on bad terms with your spouse/partner, you may need to go further and put the matter before the court. To

 The Legal Services Commission website publishes official information leaflets about legal aid: www.legalservices.gov.uk/public/help/leaflets.asp and the leaflet: A Practical Guide to Community Legal Service Funding contains up-to-date financial limits.

cover the cost of this you can apply for second-stage public funding (formerly referred to as 'full legal aid'), which itself has two levels – Approved Family Help and/or Legal Representation.

MEDIATION AND PUBLIC FUNDING

You cannot make an application for Approved Family Help and/or Legal Representation until you have first been put through a process to see whether your case would be suitable for mediation. Your solicitor will refer you to one of the locally approved mediation services. They will contact you and your ex to arrange an initial appointment. At the first appointment the mediator will explain to each of you how mediation works and explore with you whether you would want, or be able, to take it further.

The scheme recognises that there are some situations that are simply not going to be suitable for mediation: cases where there has been domestic violence, for example, or child-care cases where the local authority is involved. Also, even if you are prepared to use mediation, your spouse may refuse, in which case mediation cannot take place. If your case is not suitable (see below), the mediator will refer you back to your solicitor so that you can apply for further funding.

This process of screening for mediation inevitably delays the grant of a full certificate of public funding, if that is what you are going to need. However, try to make the most of the opportunity. See Chapter 5 for further information on mediation and its advantages.

If mediation is suitable and you work out a settlement this way then you can have legal aid (called Family Mediation) to cover the mediator's costs. Your solicitor is paid for by legal aid called Help with Mediation. Your solicitor should advise you during the mediation and will in due course put your agreement into a legally binding form.

Uniquely, you do not have to pay the statutory charge (see below) for

Solicitors' charging scales

Issue	Charging level	Hours
Children's issues only	£150	About 2 and a half
Financial issues only	£250	About 4
Children's and financial issues	£350	About 6 and a half

the work that the mediator and solicitor does and the amount that he or she is paid. This is an incentive for using the mediation route to settlement.

Help with Mediation is available only if you are taking part in family mediation or you have successfully reached an agreement and need legal advice or support from your solicitor. You can have help from a solicitor until the work that is done for you reaches a particular charging level.

If mediation is not suitable, then you need the other form of Approved Family Help legal aid: General Family Help. A General Family Help certificate will be limited to cover up to £1,500 of work. If proceedings go as far as a contested hearing, then your solicitor must get the certificate extended to cover Legal Representation, which is the second level of the second stage of public funding. Legal Representation can be granted on an emergency basis; if you need to go straight to court, the certificate will immediately cover Legal Representation.

APPLYING FOR APPROVED FAMILY HELP AND/OR LEGAL REPRESENTATION

To apply for any form of Approved Family Help and/or Legal Representation, you have to fill in two long forms. One form deals with all your financial

circumstances, in considerable detail; the other deals with the legal proceedings that you want to take. If you are in work, you will be given a third form to take to your employer so that he or she can confirm your wages. Your solicitor will help you to fill in the forms and should check that everything is correctly completed. He or she should also explain to you about the statutory charge (see below) and give you a leaflet about it.

The financial limits for Legal Help (see page 15) are not the same as those for General Family Help/Legal Representation; it is possible to be eligible for General Family Help/Legal Representation even if you are not eligible for Legal Help. If you are receiving income support or income-based jobseeker's allowance, you will automatically be eligible for General Family Help/Legal Representation without any inquiry being made into your financial circumstances.

Your completed forms are sent off to the LSC, which works out whether you are entitled to Approved Family Help/Legal Representation. It also assesses, from the information you have given on the form, whether you have a worthwhile case: the 'merits test'. If you meet these two criteria then the forms are passed to the assessment office of the Benefits Agency to check your financial circumstances.

If you qualify for Approved Family Help/Legal Representation, you may be asked to pay nothing, or a contribution towards your legal costs. This may be a one-off payment out of capital or, more likely, a regular amount each month for as long as the case takes. If you are asked to make a contribution, it is important that you ensure that you pay the amounts regularly. If you miss payments, your certificate will be taken away from you and you may have to pay for all your costs yourself. The payments are made to the LSC; you do not pay your solicitor directly. In due course, as with Legal Help, your solicitor submits his or her bill to the LSC and is paid by it. As with Legal Help, if at the end of the divorce you get or keep assets, you will have to pay back to the LSC what it has paid to your solicitor. This clawback is called the Statutory Charge (see below).

If, when you receive the assessment from the LSC, you think that the contribution that you have been asked for is too high and a mistake has been made, you can ask for the amount to be reassessed. But this will take time and delay the granting of your certificate. It is often better to pay the first instalment you have been asked to pay and get the certificate issued before asking for the contribution to be reassessed.

It can take some weeks for the LSC to process your application. If you are eligible and you are not

Contracting-out alert
You must tell the LSC if:
- There is any change in your financial circumstances.
- You stop living with your spouse/ partner.
- You start living with someone as a couple.
- You change your address.

being asked to make a contribution, you and your solicitor will hear from the LSC with a copy of your certificate. If you are asked to make a contribution, you will not get the certificate until you have accepted the offer of funding and paid the first instalment. This can hold up your case because a certificate is not retrospective in effect; the LSC will not pay your solicitor for work done on financial matters before the granting of the certificate. If you have Legal Help, then your solicitor may be able to deal with some matters within its scope, but remember that the time the solicitor can charge under Legal Help is restricted and for marriages/CPs is mostly used up in dealing with just the divorce/dissolution.

EMERGENCY APPLICATIONS

You can get Legal Representation on an emergency basis – mostly this will be used for domestic violence injunctions. Solicitors in firms that are contracted to do so

Are you entitled to legal aid and would the statutory charge apply?

Legal help

Advice at the start of your case.
Also covers undefended divorce/dissolution.

Approved family help

To get legal aid for further steps, you must first check out mediation and see if it is suitable for you.

Mediation is suitable

Not suitable

General family help

To cover negotiations and issuing court proceedings.

Family mediation

To cover the costs of mediation.

if matters go as far as a final contested hearing

and

Legal representation

To cover being represented at court.

Help with mediation

To cover the costs of the solicitor advising on the mediation and putting the agreement into a legally binding form.

Statutory charge

Applies to these forms of legal aid.

Statutory charge

DOES NOT apply to these forms of legal aid.

by the LSC can grant an emergency certificate without applying to the LSC office beforehand. Otherwise the application can be made by post/fax and granted the next day. In extreme (and rare) cases, a certificate may be granted over the telephone. An emergency certificate will cover the first stages of the work that needs to be done.

When you make the application you have to promise to make a full application and complete all the forms. You also have to promise that, if it turns out that you are not financially eligible, or you do not accept the offer when it is made to you, you will be liable for the entire cost of the case.

Your contribution to your legal aid will be reassessed if your disposable income goes up by more than £60 a

False declarations
If anybody intentionally fails to comply with legal aid regulations about information to be provided by him or her, or knowingly makes any false statement or false representation, he or she will be liable to a fine, or imprisonment for up to three months.

month, or down by more than £25 a month, or if your disposable capital goes up by more than £750. If your financial position has increased past the point where you would be eligible for funding, your certificate may be discharged (that is, stopped), so that you are then responsible for the costs of your case from that point onwards.

If the LSC decides that you have in some way misled it about your financial position, your certificate can be revoked. This means that it is treated as though it never existed. Your solicitor will then be entitled to seek to recover from you the full amount of costs he or she would have charged on a private basis, rather than the reduced fees under the legal aid certificate.

If you don't answer letters from the LSC, or you do not make the monthly repayments, your

Emergency funding

A solicitor is very unlikely to make an application for emergency funding unless he or she thinks that you will be financially eligible. It is therefore important to be very accurate about your financial circumstances when you tell the solicitor about them at the outset of your case. See Chapter 9 for Emergency Remedies.

Paying Back the Legal Service Commission: The Statutory Charge from the LSC website: www.legalservices.gov.uk/public/help/leaflets.asp

certificate can be discharged. You would then have to raise the money to pay your solicitor privately.

FINANCIAL LIMITATIONS ON LEGAL AID

Just as there are limits on the amount of work your solicitor can do under Legal Help, there are ceilings on the costs for General Family Help and Legal Representation. For General Family Help your solicitor can do work until his or her costs reach £1,500. If it looks as though the costs will mount higher than this, he or she can apply to the LSC for an extension. He or she will have to justify why this is necessary. A certificate for Legal Representation will also have a financial limit put on it. This will vary depending on what work it covers. The LSC can also put limitations on precisely what sort of legal actions your solicitor can take. Your solicitor should go through the certificate with you and explain any restrictions. Again, if more, or different, action is needed, your solicitor can justify this to the LSC and seek an extension to cover the further work.

Legal fees for someone on legal aid

If you have any form of legal aid, you stop being personally responsible for the costs of your case. Your solicitor cannot give you a bill for the work that he or she is doing for you under the certificate or ask you to pay disbursements (that is, costs and fees paid out by

"As you will not be paying your solicitor directly it is easy to forget that, as the case goes on, the costs will be mounting."

him or her on your behalf) for your case. Solicitors are not paid by the LSC at the rates that they charge their private cases. Nor are they paid for all the work that they will do. This may mean that the solicitor will not be paid to attend court on your behalf if there is a barrister instructed for you, and so may send a clerk or a trainee instead. This may be worrying for you, but in practical terms the personal presence of your solicitor may make very little difference. You cannot offer to pay an extra amount out of your own pocket for an extra service by your solicitor; he or she is not allowed to be paid by you directly when you have legal aid.

Keeping track of costs

It is important to remember that you will have to face the costs, when the statutory charge begins. Your solicitor should give you a regular (at least once every six months) update on the running total of your costs. This will have to be an estimate, because the bill will not be finalised until the end, when it is checked by the LSC

21

or the court, but it should give you a realistic idea of how the costs are increasing. It is worth remembering that costs do not tend to mount in a steady progression and can jump up suddenly; some procedures, like applications to court, are cost-intensive because they require a lot of time to be spent.

Your solicitor has a duty to keep an eye on costs for the LSC too – the LSC will not be prepared to fund litigation if it thinks that you are unreasonably escalating the costs. Your solicitor is expected to report to the LSC if he or she thinks that you are not acting reasonably. For example, if your ex makes an offer to settle the case, your solicitor, and your barrister, if you have one, will advise you on whether you should take it or incur further costs trying to increase the settlement. If you refuse to take their advice to settle a case, they will have to consider whether to refer the matter to the LSC. This may seem very unfair, but if you were paying privately, you would have to consider whether it was worth the risk of spending more of your money to achieve an outcome that might be uncertain.

THE STATUTORY CHARGE

When you sign the forms applying for public funding your solicitor should give you two leaflets: A Practical Guide to Community Legal Service Funding and Paying Back the Legal Service Commission: The Statutory Charge.

Your solicitor should also explain to you how the statutory charge works and answer any questions that you have.

The purpose of the statutory charge is to recoup some of the taxpayers' money that finances the legal aid fund. If you keep or are awarded (the Act says 'recover or preserve') any money or property, at the end of the case you will have to pay the LSC back for the costs it has paid on your behalf. It does not matter whether you get the money or property as a result of a decision by a court or an agreement with your spouse/partner. If you have already paid a contribution towards your certificate and it is more than the costs of the case, you will be entitled to a refund of the difference. More often, however, the costs will be more than you have already paid. To recover the shortfall, the LSC is allowed first call on the money or property. Even if you get an award of costs from the court at the end of your case, this does not mean that your spouse/partner will be ordered to pay your entire bill.

The charge will cover all proceedings for which you had funding. So, if your legal aid covers an injunction, negotiations about the children and the financial issues, all the costs for these three things will be rolled up together, even if you

 Maintenance payments do not count as property but all lump sums do.

22

recovered or preserved your property in only one aspect of the proceedings.

In practice, the only way of keeping any other property out of the scope of the statutory charge would be if you had reached a final agreement about it before the certificate was granted, or it was conceded that it was never a matter of dispute between you and your spouse/partner that you should have it. If this is the case, then it is sensible to tell the LSC about this at the time when you apply for a certificate, so that it knows you are not going to recover or preserve property as a result of the proceedings.

AT THE END OF YOUR CASE

Your solicitor is obliged to hold any money or property that you receive from your spouse/partner and pay it first to the LSC, so that it can take the statutory charge out of it before you receive it. If the sum that you have received from your spouse/partner is far more than the projected figure for costs, your solicitor may be permitted to release part of it to you provided he or she retains enough to cover the bill.

The immediate payment of the statutory charge would obviously cause hardship if the property is the home in which you would otherwise be living, or a sum of money intended for the purchase of a home. If this is the case, the charge can be postponed. A charge like a mortgage is put on the house and the money and accrued interest on it is repaid only when the house

is sold. Interest (at 8 per cent simple interest per year from 1 October 2005; the rate may alter) is added to the original debt. (If you do not agree to pay the interest, the LSC will not allow the charge to be postponed.) If the house is sold so that another home can be bought with the proceeds of sale, the LSC will generally agree that the charge can be put on the new home, provided the value of the new home is sufficient to cover the debt. If the charge is going to be postponed in this way, it is important that the court order or agreement records that the property is intended to be the home of the funded person, or the money is intended for the purchase of a home for the funded person.

The LSC sends annual statements to people who have charges on their homes to tell them the amount of interest that has accrued. This allows you to keep track of what you owe the LSC.

If you do not recover or preserve property at the end of your case, then the charge will not apply. This can happen in cases where there is no capital to be divided, or where there is no interest on which the LSC can take a charge. The most common example of this is where your home was rented. The settlement or court order may result in the transfer of the tenancy to one of you, but the tenancy is not something that can be charged with the debt.

Cost orders and assessment

The general principle in English law is that the loser pays the winner's costs. However, this is not consistently applied in family proceedings. The rules about costs depend on what sorts of proceedings you are involved in.

COSTS FOR DIFFERENT TYPES OF PROCEEDINGS

Even if you get an order for costs against your ex, this will not generally be for the whole of your bill. The costs may be awarded by the court on a standard basis or, (the higher level) an indemnity basis.

Unless otherwise specified, an order for costs usually means 'standard' costs. This means that you will recover, from the person ordered to pay the costs, usually between 60 and 80 per cent of your own bill. It is rare to get an order for 'indemnity costs' which means that your bill for legal costs (whether you have legal aid or not) will be met in full. When an order for costs is made and a figure cannot be agreed, the bill will be assessed. The bill should be sent to the LSC or court for assessment within three months of the date of the order for costs.

Where an order for costs is made in favour of someone who is legally aided against the other spouse/partner who is paying privately, the legally aided solicitor can claim legal fees worked out on private rates against the party ordered to pay the costs and can recoup these higher fees from him or her. The legally aided spouse/partner will not be affected directly by the fact that his or her solicitor will be able to charge extra fees, but indirectly by a reduction to the money that the family has to share. (These rules were brought in to try to stem the numbers of solicitors refusing to take on legal aid cases because of the low hourly legal aid rates.)

If someone who is legally aided is ordered to pay the other person's costs (this happens, but not very frequently), the certificate does not cover this: the person is likely to have to pay out of his or her own pocket. The court must decide the amount that is reasonable for the legally aided person to pay and will usually say that an order for costs cannot be enforced without the court's permission. It may limit the amount of such costs to the

Personal liability
It is important to remember that you are always responsible for the payment of your own solicitor's bill; if you get an order that your spouse/partner is to pay the costs, this is just to reimburse you. Your liability to the solicitor remains.

Jargon buster

Petitioner The person who asks the court for the divorce/dissolution, by filing a 'petition'.
Respondent The other spouse/cp who responds to the petition.

equivalent of the person's legal aid contributions and make the costs payable by instalments over 12 months.

DIVORCE/DISSOLUTION

The costs of the divorce/dissolution are dealt with separately from the costs of dealing with the financial side of things, or disputes about children. The petitioner can ask for costs (although this is not usual where the petition is on the basis of two years' separation with consent). If an order for costs is made, however, this does not mean that the respondent pays all the costs. The only costs that the petitioner can recover are the court fees and a limited amount towards the costs of his/her solicitor. The County Court rules set out the scales for payment. The petitioner still has to pay the difference, which may be considerable, depending on the amount of work the solicitor has done.

❝In practice, most couples agree to pay their own costs for the divorce/dissolution, or will agree a fixed contribution from the respondent.❞

For residence, contact and other orders about children

Considerable costs can be run up in disputes over orders about the children. It is rare for costs orders to be made, because it is generally difficult to say who has 'won' or who has 'lost'. The court is only likely to order someone to pay costs if his/her behaviour during the proceedings has been in some way quite unreasonable, causing unnecessary delays and expense.

Domestic abuse injunctions

Injunction proceedings can run up very substantial costs. If you get an injunction you can generally obtain an order for costs against your spouse/partner. But, in many cases, this may not be worth the paper it is written on, either because he or she disappears or because he or she has no money to pay the order.

Financial matters in divorce/dissolution

The costs rules about this changed in April 2006. The basis of the new rules is that each person's costs should be treated as part of their financial needs in the split. This means that the costs should come out of the general family assets before the court then divides the rest between them. If you get as far as a final financial hearing, your solicitors will have to bring a detailed break down of your costs to the court, so that you both know the figures involved.

Treating the costs as part of the family debts should be a powerful deterrent to running up costs in litigation, and the idea is to encourage couples to think about settlement as far as possible.

It is still possible for one person to be ordered to pay the other's costs. The judge has power to do this if he or she has not complied with a direction from the court or

Disputes over finances between cohabitants

The rules about these costs are not the same as those in divorce/dissolution. You are each responsible for your own costs and, as the court has no powers to consider your 'needs' when working out the financial order, you will only be able to get an order against your partner if you 'win' your claim. As in other proceedings, costs may be awarded against someone who has behaved unreasonably, or not complied with a court order. The court can also take into account whether you have made or received a reasonable offer to settle the claims.

has behaved unreasonably. The court can also take into account whether offers to settle the case have been made.

ᴄᴄ If one person makes a reasonable offer to settle the case and the other refuses and continues to litigate, costs might be ordered against them. ᴊᴊ

Jargon buster

Confusingly, assessment of costs used to be called 'taxation'. You may still find solicitors calling it by the old name.

ASSESSMENT

Assessment is the process whereby the district judge at the County Court (or the LSC for some legal aid bills) considers the solicitor's bill and decides whether the charges are fair and reasonable given the circumstances of the particular case. Not all bills have to go through assessment. If you agree that your solicitor's charges are fair, you will simply pay them. If your spouse/partner is ordered, or agrees, to pay part of your costs and the figure is agreed with your solicitors, the bill will not be assessed. If the figure is challenged, either by you or by your spouse/partner where there is an order for costs against him or her, then the bill will be assessed by the court.

For assessment, the bill has to be drawn up in a specially detailed form in chronological order of the steps taken. The costs of drawing up the bill, which is generally done by a specialist called a costs draftsman, are part of the costs

of case. In a legal aid case these costs will form part of the statutory charge. Your solicitor then has to submit the bill to the court and the judge goes through it, reducing any item on which he or she thinks there has been an overcharge. The bill is then returned to the solicitor and copies should go to anyone who has challenged the costs. You are entitled to a copy if you have had legal aid. You then have two choices: you can either accept the reductions made by the judge or you can challenge them. Typically, the solicitor will want to challenge the reductions by arguing that they should not have been so large. The paying party may want to challenge the reductions by arguing that there should be more of them, or that they should be increased.

If any party is not satisfied with this 'provisional' assessment, he or she can ask for a hearing and the judge then goes through the bill with all parties present.

Challenging the bill

There is a financial risk involved if you challenge your solicitor's bill, because unless you succeed in reducing the bill by at least 20 per cent, you run the risk of the costs of the assessment hearing being ordered against you.

WHEN COSTS ARE PAID

The theoretical (and usually the practical) position is if you have had an order for part of your costs to be paid, you still have to pay your solicitor's bill first, and then recover any contribution ordered by the court from your spouse/partner. Usually, your solicitor will continue to act by preparing the bill and having it assessed. If need be they will take legal steps to enforce the payment.

Sometimes the solicitor will not press you for payment of that part of the costs which are recoverable from your spouse/partner, but that is entirely a matter of the solicitor's benevolence and is based on his or her assessment of the prospect of your ex actually paying up.

Financial planning

It is important to plan ahead for the future when you are splitting up, even if you never wanted the split to happen in the first place. This doesn't mean that you have to make all the decisions at once, but you will find it helpful to work out your financial position and your options.

Your financial dossier

Organizing your finances will help you and make instructing your solicitor (if you use one) more efficient. As you start to put the financial dossier together, it is a good idea to keep the relevant documents and paperwork together in one file for quick reference.

You can use these guidelines to prepare a summary of information for your solicitor, who could then help to sort through them and assist you in planning for the future. You may not be able to work out all the figures by yourself: your ex's position may be a blank, for example. But you should still fill in as much of the picture as you can so that you understand your situation.

CAPITAL ASSETS
If you own your own home

Current Value (estimate)

How much did it originally cost?

Is the home in joint names?

(You can get this information via the Land Registry website: www.landregisteronline.gov.uk or a solicitor can do it for you.)

How did you arrange your finances to pay for it? Who put down the deposit, and where did the money come from?

If you own a leasehold property (that is, with a long lease, usually of 25 years or more):

What is the ground rent?

What is the service/maintenance charge (if there is one)?

How long is the lease?

If you have a mortgage:

Write down the details of the building society, bank or other lender:

      Name

      Address

      Account/reference number

How much is outstanding?

What are the monthly payments?

When will it be paid off?

If it's an endowment mortgage:

When is the policy due to mature and for how much?

What is the current surrender/paid-up value of the policy? (Include details of any occupational pensions, superannuation schemes and personal plans (including, from April 2001, stakeholder schemes) to which you belong.)

Pensions

Does the pension scheme or plan provide any benefits for a widower or widow or dependent cohabitant?

What is the value of the pension you expect to receive on retirement?

What is the Cash Equivalent Transfer Value (CETV) of your pension?

Vehicles (cars, caravans, motorcycles).

Other assets

Any joint current accounts or savings accounts you have with details of the account(s) and current balance(s).

Your own savings in building society, bank or National Savings accounts, with details of account(s) and current balance(s).

Stocks, shares, and unit trusts, with a current valuation of holdings.

Personal Equity Plans (PEPs), Tax-Exempt Special Savings Accounts (TESSAs), Individual Savings Accounts (ISAs) or other investments.

Endowment policies and/or life insurance policies:

> how much are they worth now?

> when do they mature?

(You could ask the insurance company/broker for current surrender values and check if any policy has been written in your ex's favour.)

Valuables (like jewellery, antiques) with estimates of their value and brief details of how/by which of you they were acquired.

Are you and/or your spouse likely to come into an inheritance in the foreseeable future?

Does either of you have interests under a trust (perhaps as a result of tax planning by you or your parents)?

Details of future assets (demutualisation payments from a building society/insurance company, or the maturing of an insurance policy).

DEBTS

	My debt	Joint debt
n this section you can work out any large debts that you may owe on your own account or jointly with your ex.		
Loans secured on your home:		
Amount borrowed		
Outstanding balanceDate repayment should end		
Other loans or hire purchase:		
Amount borrowed		
Outstanding balance		
Date repayment should end		
Bank overdraft:		
Bank		
Amount overdrawn		
Credit cards:		
Card		
Balance		
Other debts including tax arrears		

INCOME AND OUTGOINGS

Here you can work out what your monthly income is from all sources.

Income

	Before tax/NI	Take home
From employment:		
Normal weekly or monthly earnings		
Bonuses		
Hours worked (full or part-time)		
	Gross income	Net income
From self-employment:		
What do you normally earn?		
(You should get together your last 3 years' accounts and tax returns as proof of the figures.)		

Maintenance

How much maintenance (if any) do you get from a former partner for you or for children?

Do you get maintenance from anyone else? If so, how much?

Other unearned income

- Interest
- Bonuses
- Pensions
- Other

Your state benefits

Child benefit, including lone parent benefit

Jobseeker's allowance

Income support

Working tax credit

Child tax credit

State pension

Incapacity benefit or other disability benefits

Add up all the figures above so that you can work out how much you have to spend each month.

List of outgoings (monthly)

If you are working from weekly figures, do remember that there are 4.33 weeks in each month; if you simply multiply a weekly figure by 4 you will end up leaving 4 weeks out of your annual total.

Item

Property Costs

Mortgage/rent

Endowment policy linked to mortgage

Council tax

Water rates

Electricity and gas

Service charge

Ground rent

Oil/Solid fuel

Household Expenses

Food/housekeeping

House and contents insurance

Repairs/service contracts

TV licence

List of outgoings (monthly) contd.

Telephone/broadband charges

Pets

Other Property

Second property/holiday home

Vehicles (including company vehicles if applicable)

Insurance

Road tax

Maintenance

Fuel

Children

Clothing

Books and toys

Childminder/nursery/nanny (gross cost)

Baby food/equipment

Doctor/dentist/optician

School expenses

Fees

Travel to school

School dinners

Uniform

Private lessons

After school clubs (sports, music etc)

Personal expenses

Clothes and shoes

Entertainment

Travel to work

Holidays (including the children)

Legal costs/legal aid contribution

Doctor / dentist / optician

Prescription charges

Other items

Total

Financial checklist

Use this page to summarize all the financial information that you have got together and give yourself an overview of your present position.

	Mine	Joint
Assets		
Home		
Savings and investments		
Vehicles		
Other valuables		
Debts		
Secured on house		
Unsecured		
A Total of assets		
B Total of debts		

Net assets (Figure A minus Figure B.)

Net monthly income
Earned
Benefits
Unearned

C Total
D Monthly outgoings

Net shortfall/surplus
(Figure C minus figure D.)

Planning ahead

Once you have a record of your present financial position you can think about how to manage once you separate. Not all items will change. If you have made plans for a new home, try making a list with the projected figures for that home. It is also helpful to do the same exercise for your ex (as far as you can). If your plan is sensible, you can take steps to reduce the potentially crippling financial fallout from splitting up.

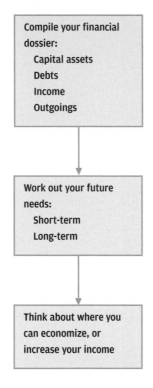

Compile your financial dossier:
- Capital assets
- Debts
- Income
- Outgoings

Work out your future needs:
- Short-term
- Long-term

Think about where you can economize, or increase your income

Retirement plans
You are taking a big gamble with your retirement income if you take no steps to protect yourself against the effects of inflation. Options include saving in early retirement to top up your pension later on or choosing an annuity which increases each year.

WHERE TO LIVE

Your first priority, if you have children, will of course be to ensure that they have a roof over their heads. Work out what it would cost you to stay on in your home, and where you could move to if you were to move, and how either option would leave you and your ex financially.

Once you have found out the value of the home, deduct the likely agent's and conveyancing costs and moving costs (say, about 5 per cent of the house value),

“ Suddenly you've got to make what supported one household stretch to two. ”

Future plans
Making plans for the future always revolves primarily around accommodation and income.

❝ Factors such as the location of children's schools and being near to helpful friends or parents can be important, especially now that you are going to be on your own. **❞**

plus what you owe on the mortgage, and you are left with the 'net equity'. Out of the net amount, you would have to pay the costs of setting up a new home or possibly two – one for each of you. Work out what sort of mortgage you and your ex could each take on and then investigate the property market.

If you are in rented accommodation, and indeed even if you are not, investigate the rented sector – private, council and housing association.

This can be a disheartening business at the best of times, but it is only by exploring what might be possible that you can work out what the options are, and the respective advantages and disadvantages of each option.

WHAT TO LIVE ON

If you have worked out your net income and your outgoings you will know whether you have

Working out maintenance

If you have dependent children, first work out how much child support might be payable under the formula laid down by the Child Support Acts. Turn to Chapter 6 to work out how much child support is likely to be payable.

enough to live on or (more likely) whether there is going to be a deficit each month. You need to also consider the changes that will occur when you are apart. If you have children you will need to work out how much you might expect to receive or pay in maintenance for them. You also need to consider how your new status as a single person might affect any benefits to which you are entitled. Spouses/cps

You could perhaps think of renting out a room to a lodger – under the 'rent a room scheme' you can receive up to £4,250 per year tax free (2006-7 figures). Further information is on the HMRC website.*

can also claim maintenance for themselves though this tends not to happen if you are both working. These figures need adding into your calculations.

MAXIMIZE YOUR INCOME

In addition to maintenance, you may be able to take steps to include your earned income. Tax credits and benefits will change once you move from being part of a couple to being single. You should tell your payroll department as soon as possible once you have finally split up, and notify HMRC, so that you can begin to claim the benefits that you are entitled to.

If you have not been working, you may need to find a job. The most helpful benefits are available to you if you work at least 16 hours a week, so it is sensible to see if you can find a job that offers this as a minimum.

WILLS

You need to review your wills when you split up to ensure that they cover your new circumstances (if you have not already made a will, now is the time to do so). The reason for this is that if you do not make a will your estate will have to be divided according to the 'intestacy rules' and may not go to the people you want to have it. Cohabiting partners have no rights to inherit from each other.

This only applies to married/cp couples
A parent who is looking after children and therefore not working may be able to claim maintenance for herself/himself to top up child support. A spouse/civil partner who does not work outside the home or who is on a low income may also be entitled to spousal maintenance from the other spouse/cp if he/she earns enough. Exactly how much maintenance is not easy to quantify as the court will take a number of factors into account. If sufficient income is available a non-working spouse/cp can expect to receive not only enough to meet reasonable needs but also a clear proportion of the other's earnings. The court will generally expect a spouse/cp who is not currently earning to make sensible attempts to be self-supporting in the future.

It should be added that there is no gender bias in the statute law. However, women often earn less than their male counterparts and maintenance awards may compensate for this.

Conversely, your spouse/cp remains your next of kin until you are finally divorced and would inherit from you if you die while the divorce was pending.

TYPES OF WILL

Check whether your will is a 'mutual will' – in which case you need to change it quickly. A mutual will is a legal term used to describe wills made by a couple which complement each other and which are made on the basis that the first one to die binds the survivor to make a will in the original agreed format – no changes will be allowed. Mutual wills are rare – they are not the same as the more common 'mirror wills', whereby a couple agree to make similar wills, which can be changed whenever one person wants. If a mutual will is to be changed, it must be changed before the other person's death.

This only applies to married/cp couples

A will made by a spouse/cp is not automatically revoked on divorce (or even an annulment of the marriage), but is interpreted as if the ex had died on the date of the divorce (or annulment). So if the ex was named as an executor, that appointment will not take place, and the same applies to an appointment of an ex as guardian of the children – unless there is any contrary intention expressed in the will. The gift in a will of any property to an ex will fail as well.

WHY MAKE A WILL?

There are significant advantages to making a will. As long as you have made a will, the rest of the world will know what you want to happen after your death. If your priority is to ensure that the children are cared for after your death, by making a will you can be reasonably certain that your wishes will be carried out. If someone else has parental responsibility with you (this is generally the case if you are married/cp), and you die, the other person will legally have sole responsibility for the children. If you are the sole parent with PR, there will be no-one legally responsible for the children until the court appoints a guardian. It is up to you to say who should care for the children. You should think about who you would want to have day to day care of the children and who you would want to

Legal help making a will

You can ask for advice under the Legal Help scheme for preparing your will if you meet all the financial criteria listed in Chapter 1 and:
- are a single parent looking after a child and you want to appoint a guardian for the child to act after death, or
- are aged 70 or over, or
- are disabled, or
- have a child who is disabled.

look after money or property for them;
this isn't necessarily the same person.
Make sure that you do discuss the
responsibility with the people you
intend to appoint in your will.

 This only applies to married/cp couples

Preventing disposal of assets If you
strongly suspect that your spouse/cp is
intending to dispose of assets to try to
escape his or her financial obligations, do
bear in mind the following:
• You can ask the court to make an
  application under Section 37 of the
  Matrimonial Causes Act to prevent him
  or her from doing so.
• To do this, you will need to instruct a
  solicitor (see Chapter 7).
• This can be done as an emergency
  application if necessary.
• You should not delay if you think that
  you need to make such an application.

 For more detailed information on wills see *Which? Essential Guide Wills and Probate.*

Financial help from the state

Financial help from the state may seem rather off-putting, especially if you once thought that you were not the sort of person who would have to turn to state help at any stage in your life. However, you should check your entitlement; such support could be vital.

The types of benefit that you may be eligible to apply for are:

- Child benefit and Child tax credit
- Income support
- Jobseeker's allowance
- Working tax credit
- Housing benefit
- Council tax benefit
- Loans from the social fund

If you receive jobseeker's allowance or income support, you will automatically be entitled to legal aid (see Chapter 1). It is helpful, therefore (though not always possible), to get your benefits position sorted out before you consult a solicitor.

INCOME SUPPORT

Income support is available to lone parents who are looking after children under 16. You must be not working, or working fewer than 16 hours per week.

You can visit, write to or phone your local Jobcentre Plus or social security office and you will be issued with a claim form, which you can also download from the DWP website. You will be asked to attend an interview with a Personal Adviser. You are obliged to attend this interview if you want to claim benefit. Failure to do so may result in the loss of benefit but you do not have to seek work as a result of the meeting. Information about these meetings is available from your local office, or you can download it from the DWP website. The government's New Deal for Lone Parents, which is set out in detail in the booklet, provides a number of extra allowances for lone parents, with incentives and help intended to get you into work. They are too detailed to be set out at length in this book.

 Help and advice on benefits are available from your local social security office, and from the Department for Work and Pensions (DWP) helplines. You can also download information leaflets from the DWP's website www.dwp.gov.uk

To be eligible for income support, your capital must be worth less than £16,000 (but this does not include the value of your home). The amount that you get depends on your age and on the age of the children living with you, as well as any other income that you have coming into the house.

If you are a lone parent, £20 of your earnings or income will be ignored if you are working under 16 hours a week. The first £6,000 of capital is ignored. If your capital is worth between £6,000.01 and £16,000 (inclusive), what you receive by way of income support will be affected by the assumption that you have a weekly income of £1 for every £250 (or part of £250) over £6,000.

If you are a lone parent in receipt of income support, the Child Support Agency (CSA) will insist that you make an application for child support via the Agency against the child(ren)'s other parent (see Chapter 6). This requirement will end when the new rules come into effect. You can keep up to £10 a week of any maintenance paid without your benefit being correspondingly reduced. This is called the Child Maintenance Premium.

Help with the mortgage

If you pay a mortgage, you can have some help with the interest, but not the capital repayments. The amount that you receive depends on when you bought your house. If you bought your house and your present mortgage was taken out before the beginning of October 1995, you will not receive any interest at all for the first eight weeks. Then you get 50 per cent of the interest for a further 18 weeks and only after that 100 per cent of the interest. If you bought your house and took out the mortgage after 1 October 1995, you receive no help at all with the interest until 39 weeks have gone past, but then you get 100 per cent. (If you are aged over 60, the waiting period does not apply.) The maximum mortgage loan taken into account is £100,000. Payments on a loan above that figure will not be met by the DWP. This is only a brief summary of the rules, which are complicated. The DWP publishes a helpful leaflet (IS8), and the benefits office will give you precise advice about your own situation.

If your mortgage does not qualify for help, you may be covered by the terms of an insurance policy. You will need to check the terms of the policy carefully; most cover redundancy but

 Details of the government's New Deal scheme are also available on the web at www.newdeal.gov.uk

not family breakdown. Moreover, most policies do not kick in immediately, and may run only for a fixed period, such as two years.

JOBSEEKER'S ALLOWANCE

Jobseeker's allowance is another state benefit you may be eligible for. To qualify, you must be unemployed or working on average fewer than 16 hours per week. If you work part-time and are a lone parent, the first £20 of your earnings is disregarded.

To apply, get a claim pack from your local Jobcentre Plus or social security office. This has the claim form in it along with a Jobsearch Plan. You will have to attend an interview and take the forms with you. The interviewer draws up a Jobseeker's Agreement with you.

The rates at which the benefit is paid are the same as for income support and you will qualify for housing benefit and council tax benefit as well.

CHILD TAX CREDIT AND WORKING TAX CREDIT

These two tax credits support families with children, and working people on low incomes. All families with children can claim. You can get a tax credit if your joint income

❝ Income support claimants are also entitled to help with the costs of rent or mortgage, but this has its limitations. ❞

is up to about £50,000, and rather more if you have a baby under 12 months old. You can check your eligibility on the HM Customs and Revenue (HMRC) website.

You do not have to work to claim child tax credit. If you are not in work, the child tax credit is paid in addition to any income support or jobseeker's allowance that you are entitled to for yourself. Child tax credit is paid for children up to 16 and for 16–18-year-olds who are in school. Children aged 16–17 who have left school, are not yet working and have signed on with Connexions or the Careers Service also qualify. Only the family with the main responsibility for the children can claim the credit, so if the children's time is divided fairly evenly between both parents, you will need to negotiate this. HMRC has said that it will decide who is entitled to the credit if there is a dispute.

In addition to child tax credit you can claim working tax credit if you

Go to www.hmrc.gov.uk for general information on tax credits.
www.hmrc.gov.uk/menus/credits.htm for the tax credit information page

are working 16 hours or more a week and have the responsibility for at least one child. If you don't have children and are over 26 you must work at least 30 hours a week. You can claim an element of child-care costs if they are provided by a 'registered' or 'approved' scheme. Your capital is generally disregarded unless it produces an income for you. Income is generally taken into account only if it is taxable, so maintenance payments whether voluntary or via the CSA will not count. If you are entitled to these tax credits you can also claim a range of other fringe benefits such as free dental care and prescriptions. The HMRC Leaflet WTC6 sets these out in full.

HOUSING BENEFIT

Housing benefit is available if you are living in rented accommodation. If you claim income support or jobseeker's allowance, you can claim housing benefit at the same time via the DWP. Otherwise, you make the claim to your local authority.

If your landlord is the local authority, the amount of rent will be reduced directly. If you pay to a private landlord, the benefit is paid by cheque or money order. It is assessed for a period of up to 60 weeks at a time, but may be shorter if your tenancy ends during that period, or if the local authority has other arrangements. The maximum that you can get is 100 per cent of the 'eligible rent', which is not necessarily the amount that you pay to your landlord. You will need to get detailed advice from your local benefit office or from the CAB about the calculation.

COUNCIL TAX BENEFIT

If you claim income support or jobseeker's allowance, you can claim council tax benefit at the same time. The maximum that you can get is the whole of your council tax bill. If your house is in valuation bands F, G or H, you will have your benefit restricted to the amount payable for a property in band E.

As for housing benefit, if you have more money coming in than the allowances and premiums that you qualify for under DWP regulations you will receive less council tax benefit.

Loans from the social fund

If you have been receiving income support or jobseeker's allowance for at least 26 weeks, you may be able to get payments from the social fund for items of capital expenditure which would be too large to meet out of your income. There are different kinds of loan. To spread the payment for an exceptional expense you could get a 'budgeting loan'. These are for sums between £100 and £1,500. Any award is reduced by capital over £1,000. The loan is interest-free, but is repayable and is usually made over a period of up to 78 weeks with the repayments coming out of the benefit paid.

You can also get a 'crisis loan' for expenses in an emergency or as a consequence of a disaster, if there is no other way of meeting the needs. The fund officer at the DWP will want to be satisfied that the loan is the only means of preventing serious damage or serious risk to the health or safety of you or your family. Social fund loans come out of a fixed budget; if the fund has reached its limit for the year, your application may be refused on these grounds alone.

Figures and forecast

Once you have worked out what money will be available, compare the figures with a forecast for the needs of both new households. This may show that one of you has, or both of you have, nowhere near enough to meet your projected expenses. Remember that the needs of the children will take priority.

To work out your capital, look at your summary of assets (on page 35), having worked out the net equity in the house (if you own it) and the net value of all other

If you have more money coming in than the allowances and premiums that you qualify for under DWP regulations, you will receive less housing benefit.

realisable assets after you have paid any debts (including legal fees for the divorce, if you are consulting a solicitor).

You may need to think about turning some of your assets into cash (realising them). What is realisable will depend upon your circumstances – cashing in a life insurance policy or selling the car might be foolish in some circumstances but unavoidable in others. Everyday household belongings are rarely realisable and should preferably be linked to need: the parent with the children, for example, is likely to need the washing machine and the majority of the furnishings. The other parent, however, may need to buy, either immediately or in due course, his or her own household equipment and furniture. You may be able to rent some appliances, such as a washing machine, if the capital outlay is too much at first.

Looking at your incomes, needs and available capital (if any), you will have to decide how things can be arranged, but with realistic figures. In many cases, you will have to accept that both of you are going to be very hard up, at least for a while.

Managing debts

Getting into debt has become a common problem. For many families, the financial issues involved in a split are less about dividing up assets than about dealing with the heavy burden of debts and who will or should take them on. Often, the stresses caused by financial debts can themselves be the cause of the family break-up.

WHO IS RESPONSIBLE?

Broadly speaking, a spouse/partner will not be responsible for debts incurred by the other spouse/partner alone. But there are exceptions: a spouse/partner will usually be responsible for the other's unpaid council tax bills and sometimes other outgoings on the home. You also share responsibility for joint debts, say from a joint account, or for joint mortgage repayments or rent.

If your spouse/partner has left the home leaving behind high unpaid household bills, the date of separation is important. If he or she has failed to pay the council tax, you must inform the local authority of the date of separation and thus at least cut off your responsibility for paying your spouse/partner's share of the council tax debt accruing after that. Your council tax bill will also be reduced if there is now only one adult living in the home. By advising the gas, electricity and telephone companies, you can also get the meters read as near to the separation date as possible and ask for a transfer of the accounts into your own name. This will, obviously, leave you with having to pay future bills and so may not be appropriate, but it can be one way of avoiding responsibility for some previously built-up debts.

If on the other hand you are paying maintenance to your ex, but he or she is not paying the bills, this leaves you in a difficulty. As long as your name is on the

For further advice about debts, try contacting the National Debtline www.nationaldebtline.co.uk You can also find advice from the Office of Fair Trading www.oft.gov.uk and the Council of Mortgage Lenders www.cml.org.uk

account, the primary responsibility is yours. If the agreement is that your ex will pay the bills, make sure that the accounts are transferred into his or her name.

WORKING OUT DEBT REPAYMENTS

The first step is to assess the priority of debts with the help of expert counselling. You will probably be advised not simply to pay off the creditor who shouts the loudest.

Don't avoid debt

Although it may be tempting to try to avoid your creditors, you may well find that by contacting them and showing that you are willing to try to repay them you can work out a realistic level of repayment.

Also, it will be less expensive for them to agree a repayment with you than to incur extra legal costs in having to take you to court.

If things go too far

If you find it impossible to pay off your debts or to repay a creditor you owe over £750, you could ask the court to make a bankruptcy order. If you take this

action yourself it will cost you a deposit of £325 plus court fees of £150.

There is an exemption from the fee if you are on income support or income-based jobseeker's allowance, or are getting the maximum working families' tax credit. Check with the court for details. You will thus largely be relieved of the burden of your

❝ Creditors will very often accept a reduced payment made regularly rather than nothing at all, and will feel happier knowing that you have not fled the country. ❞

creditors.

However, once you are made bankrupt, there are limitations: you cannot hold a bank account or obtain credit of over £500 without disclosing your bankruptcy, nor be a company director (or a solicitor, for example). Depending on the circumstances, most bankrupts are

For further information on bankruptcy, see the helpful government website: www.insolvency.gov.uk

discharged after two or three years, when they have a clean sheet.

But even if you think this is the only way out of your debts, obtain legal advice before going ahead.

Joint accounts and credit cards

With a joint bank or building-society account on which either of you can draw, there is the risk that the account could be cleared out by one of you without the other knowing about it. To prevent this, you can ask the bank or building-society manager to change the arrangement so that cheques can be drawn only with both signatures. Alternatively, you could ask for the account to be frozen (although then neither of you would be able to draw out funds).

Similarly, where each of you has a credit card or cash-withdrawal card for drawing against one account, it is usually wiser, from the main cardholder's point of view, to put a stop on the cards.

You must tell the card company and send back the cards (including, if possible, spouse/partner's card). A new card will then be issued to the main cardholder.

Your rights and the family home

If you are considering a divorce, you should think about whether you need to protect your interest in the family home, as a precautionary measure. After all, it will almosy certainly be your biggest asset.

 Home rights only apply to married/cp couples.

HOME RIGHTS

Home rights are in essence short-term rights which exist while the marriage/cp lasts (until the final decree of divorce). The long-term decisions about the rights to live in the home, or to get a share of the proceeds if it is sold, will have to be made as part of the divorce financial settlement. If violence has been threatened or used against you, making it unsafe for you to live in the family home, you can apply to the court to protect yourself (as described in Chapter 7) and sometimes gain an occupation order which can exclude your spouse/cp or allow you to re-enter the home. The courts will also be able to make an occupation order overriding a person's home rights.

Home rights

The spouse/cp who does not legally own the family home – that is, whose name is not on the title deeds – has certain 'home rights':

- The right not to be evicted without a court order if he or she is in occupation.
- The right (if the court thinks fit) to return to the home if he or she has left it.
- The right (if the court thinks fit) to exclude the owner spouse/cp from occupying the home for a period (usually only when violence has occurred).

The same occupation rights apply if the home is rented. And also apply to a property which the couple intended to use as their home but which they never actually occupied.

REGISTERING HOME RIGHTS: OWNER-OCCUPIED HOMES

If you are a joint owner of the family home, you do not need to register your home rights separately. Third parties (for example, a potential buyer or mortgagee) will become aware of your interest when they carry out a search of the property title, so your spouse/cp cannot try to sell or mortgage the property without your consent.

If, however, your spouse, not you, is the sole owner of the family home, you must register your home rights to ensure that they are protected against third parties.

How you register your home rights depends on whether the title to the family home is 'registered' or 'unregistered'.

If the title is registered

The district Land Registry for your area will advise you how to register your matrimonial home rights and should provide the various forms and tell you about the procedure.

If the title is unregistered

You should apply to register an entry against your spouse/cp's name. The form to be used, K2, is available from law stationers' shops and the fee for registration is £1 per name.

The information required includes the full name in which the property-owning spouse/cp bought or acquired the property. If you are unsure of the precise name shown on the documents, register the charge against all

The easiest way to check if the home is registered is to use the Land Registry online website www.landregisteronline.gov.uk

possible permutations; for example – John Smith, J Smith, John Peter Smith, J P Smith. The charge is ineffective unless it is in exactly the right name. If you are in any doubt, or time is short, apply to register at both the Land Registry and the Land Charges Department until you have sorted out the position. If you find that the title is registered, you should cancel the charge at the Land Charges Department.

IF YOU REGISTER A CHARGE OR NOTICE

Anyone buying the property or granting a mortgage on it would, as a matter of routine, check the appropriate registry and discover your notice or charge protecting your rights. (Even if a buyer or mortgagee does not actually search the register or has no knowledge of the registration, the effect of registering a land charge or notice amounts in law to notice of a non-owning spouse/cp's home rights.) If the house is then bought or mortgaged, this is done subject to your home rights and the buyer or mortgagee cannot turn you out unless you have agreed to give up your rights.

The effect of registration normally ceases once a decree of divorce is made final. If the question of the family home has not been settled by then, the non-owning spouse/cp should ask the court, before the decree is made final, for the registration of the class F land charge or the notice to be renewed after the final decree. Alternatively, if you are making a claim for a share of a property, you should register a 'pending action' claim, which similarly puts third parties on notice of your interest.

FINDING OUT IF YOUR SPOUSE/CP OWNS A SECOND HOME

Sometimes there may be good reason to suspect that your spouse/cp has bought another home – say if he or she has moved in with a new partner in a newly bought home which he or she says belongs to the new partner. You can now easily check this on the Land Registry online site, if you have the address.

If your suspicions are confirmed and your spouse/cp is shown as a legal owner, once you have made financial claims in the divorce proceedings you may also be able

 Protecting Matrimonial Home Rights under the Family Law Act 1996 (PG004) from HM Land Registry www.landregistry.gov.uk gives detailed information and instructions about protecting your home rights.

to register a 'pending action' claim on the title of the second property if you think that your spouse/cp may try to sell it to avoid paying money.

MOVING OUT

If you hope eventually to have the home to live in permanently, it is tactically best to try to stay there, if possible. Even if you are not planning to remain in the long term but want to persuade your spouse/cp to make other financial provisions for you, staying put may help you in your negotiations. However, the strategy of staying put can sometimes be counterproductive: remaining at close quarters with your spouse/cp once the decision to separate has been made can give rise to tensions which may undermine the prospect of successful negotiations. It may be helpful to discuss with your solicitor the pros and cons of moving out, whether on a temporary or permanent basis.

It may be tempting, if the situation between you and your spouse/cp has become very volatile, to lock him/her out of the home while he or she is away. Remember, however, that your spouse/cp has home rights, that is, a right to occupy the home, at least while the marriage is in being, and can apply to the court for an order restoring to him or her the right to occupy the home.

 This section applies to all couples who are joint owners.

SEVERING A JOINT TENANCY

If you own your home (or any other land or buildings) jointly, you need to check whether the ownership is held under a 'joint tenancy' or a 'tenancy in common'. If you have a mortgage, ask your lender. If you do not, you will need to look at the title deeds or the Land Certificate. Ask a solicitor to check the point for you.

Some solicitors advise married/cp couples to end a joint tenancy and, pending a financial settlement or a court order, divide your respective

Jargon buster

Joint tenancy Under a joint tenancy, each person's interest in the property is not quantified: you own the whole of the house (or flat) jointly. When one of you dies, the whole property automatically passes to the survivor, irrespective of any provision the former may have made in a will.

Tenancy in common Under a tenancy in common, on the other hand, the interests of each person are fixed (usually on a 50:50 basis, but it can be in any proportion) and separate, so that each person can separately dispose of his or her share by will.

interests in the property by becoming tenants in common. This will not affect your day-to-day status as co-owners but if one of you dies, the deceased's share of the property would be part of his/her estate, distributed under the terms of his/her will or according to the rules of intestacy.

If you are married/cp, the intestacy rules make your spouse/cp your next of kin until the final decree of divorce. If you are not married your partner will never be treated as your next of kin.

However, there is also the risk that if your spouse/cp were to die in the meantime, you would lose the chance that you would have had of inheriting his/her share of the home when it was held under a joint tenancy.

You will have to weigh up the risks both for and against – there is no clear-cut right or wrong course of action applicable to all. Whether it would be in your interest to sever the joint tenancy is something you should first discuss with a solicitor. If you do decide to sever the tenancy either of you can do this by sending a 'notice of severance' to the other owner at any time. A notice of severance will convert your ownership into a tenancy in common.

A notice of severance

The notice can simply take the form of a letter stating: 'Please accept this letter as notice of my desire to sever as from this day the joint tenancy in our property known as [insert address of property] now held by us as joint tenants both at law and in equity so that henceforth the said property shall belong to us as tenants in common in equal shares.' You should sign and date the letter.

 If you sever a tenency, you must make a will stating where you want your share of the property to go.

Sorting out finances

Once divorce proceedings have been filed, a raft of financial remedies is available to either spouse/cp in the form of orders for maintenance and capital payments. The orders are more limited before a divorce is filed, but remedies do exist and, in the absence of an agreement between you and your spouse/cp, you can use these, or the court, to get money on an interim basis. Cohabiting couples can also make separation agreements.

The alternatives available to you are:
- agreed arrangements, which can be informal, or formalised in a separation agreement, or
- in the absence of agreements, remedies for you (a magistrates' court order or county court order) and your children, whether they are with your spouse/cp's children (a CSA assessment) or they are your spouse/cp's stepchildren (a Children Act order or order linked to your order in the magistrates' or county court).

INFORMAL AGREED ARRANGEMENTS

Many couples manage to separate successfully and to agree who will pay for what, including the maintenance for any children. If you can do this, you do not need to have a formal agreement or an order (unless you are on benefit, in which case the CSA may insist that you use its services to obtain an order against the 'non-resident parent' (see Chapter 6), but you will be aware that there is no way of enforcing the payments if the payer is unreliable. Most such arrangements are on a short-term basis only, and it may seem unduly complicated and costly (if lawyers are involved) to formalise the agreement in a written separation agreement.

However, if the separation is going to be long term, for instance, if you propose to separate for two years and then divorce on this basis, it is probably a good idea to draw up a separation agreement. This not only makes the arrangement more certain, but you can enforce the agreement using the courts if your spouse/cp defaults.

Cohabitants can use separation agreements as well as married/cp couples, but they tend to be less common. This is because there is no right to adult maintenance if you are unmarried and therefore a maintenance arrangement between the couple is pretty rare.

Formal separation agreements

Separation agreements are sometimes referred to as 'deeds'. Technically, a legal document is a deed if it is made 'under seal'. There is no longer a requirement for little round red stickers to be put on the document, but your signatures must be formally witnessed. The document should generally be drawn up as a deed if 'real' property (houses and land) is being transferred between you, or if it contains a financial obligation that you might later want to enforce.

To ensure that a separation agreement does have effective legal force it should be made only once you are both sure that you know all about each other's financial position: what you earn, you own and you owe. It would be sensible for you each to consult a solicitor and ask the solicitor to draft the agreement. A mediation service can also help you to negotiate the terms of the agreement.

Separation agreements are usually fairly flexible and are designed to cover the particular things that you want to deal with. A typical deed will probably cover the following issues:

- That you have decided you want to live separately, and the date on which the separation started

(this date is useful for tax purposes and also for later evidence to the court of the period of your separation).

- Agreements about where and with which parent the children will make their main home. You can also deal with contact arrangements if you want them fixed, or simply express a joint intention that contact will be frequent, and state whether or not the children will stay overnight.
- Who is going to live in the family home, or whether it is going to be sold and how the proceeds are going to be divided.
- Who is going to pay for what in the future.
- Maintenance for the children.
- (For married/cp couples) maintenance from one spouse/cp to the other.
- Division of contents of the family home.
- Ownership of other assets such as the car.

If you are married/cp the agreement can also contain an expression of your intention about whether there will eventually be divorce proceedings.

Although part of the reason for making a separation agreement is to avoid being unduly legalistic, you need to make sure that anything you agree to will not have unwanted long-term consequences. Transfers of property or large assets at this stage may have implications for Capital Gains Tax. All the financial arrangements may be considered by the courts (in later divorce proceedings for instance). You need to take legal advice as to whether you are making a commitment that you will later want removed and whether a court would do so.

Most people would like to think that the separation agreement would remove the possibility of any later legal argument in court. But, if you are married/cp the court will not let its powers of making orders be removed by private agreement, so you cannot make a binding promise that you will never invoke the power of the court at a later stage. However, the courts will be inclined to uphold an agreement that both parties have made if they both had legal advice at the time that they made it and the financial disclosure on both sides had been full and frank.

If one of you does not keep to the separation agreement, it is possible to go to the court to enforce the agreement. This does not happen very often, but it can be done.

MAINTENANCE FOR A SPOUSE OR CIVIL PARTNER

If an agreement about maintenance is breached, it may be easier to make a court application for maintenance as outlined below. This, in itself, is probably enough sanction to encourage most people to keep to the arrangements that they have agreed together.

Magistrates' court – Family Proceedings Panel

You can apply to the magistrates' court for maintenance for yourself and a lump sum order up to £1,000. There is no limit on the amount of maintenance that the court can order. You can also apply more than once for a lump sum – there is no limit on the number of applications in the legislation. The court can also order a lump-sum payment, of up to £1,000, for each child.

You can make this application yourself; you do not have to have a solicitor to help you. If you are eligible for Legal Help (see Chapter 1), your solicitor can assist you with this. You can go to the court to get the application form yourself and the court staff will help you to fill it in, but they cannot give you legal advice. No fee is charged for this. There is a straightforward form on which you set out your financial position. In order to qualify for an order you have to establish that your spouse/cp:

- has failed to provide reasonable maintenance for you or to make a proper contribution towards the children of the family (see below) or
- has deserted you, or behaved in such a way that you cannot reasonably be expected to live

with him (such behaviour could include adultery).

Once you have made your 'complaint', the court will fix a day for the hearing and issue a summons to your spouse/cp, who has to be given at least 21 days' notice of the hearing.

If you manage to agree a maintenance order before, or at the hearing, the court will make an order in those terms, provided it seems to be appropriate. If the order is agreed, a capital sum can be ordered that is more than the £1,000 limit. If you cannot agree, the court will hear evidence from both of you about your financial positions and will then order what it thinks is a reasonable sum.

Normally you will have to wait between one and two months for the hearing to come to court. If you need an order more urgently than this, you should explain this to the court when you make the 'complaint' and the court can be asked to fix an expedited hearing, or to make an interim order to tide you over till a full hearing can be given. An interim order can last for a maximum of three months, which should give time for a full hearing to take place.

The county court

The alternative to the magistrates' court - and this traditionally makes orders which are rather on the low side - is to make an application to

the county court under s.27 of the Matrimonial Causes Act (CP: Sch.15, Part 8 CP 2004). The fee for this is £200. You have to satisfy the court that your spouse/cp has failed to provide reasonable maintenance for you. The application must be accompanied by a sworn statement setting out your resources and needs.

In theory legal aid should be available for such an application, but the Legal Services Commission (LSC) will probably want you to use the magistrates' court if at all possible as the costs are lower, so your solicitor will have to justify why the county court would be preferable.

You, or your solicitor, will have to serve your spouse/cp with the application and your statement. He or she, in turn, should file a financial statement in reply within 14 days of receiving yours. The court will fix a hearing, which will be heard in private.

The court procedure described in Chapter 10 will apply to a s.27 application as well. This means that there will be a First Appointment and a Financial Dispute Resolution Appointment (see Chapter 10 for details) if the case proceeds.

Given the length of time that an s.27 application takes, and its cost, it is probably not a good idea to make it unless you know that you are going to have a long-term separation and that no divorce is contemplated for the time being. Otherwise you are simply going to duplicate the proceedings and run up the costs bill.

Child Support Agency

Once you have separated, to the point where your spouse/cp is not living in the same household as the children, the CSA has jurisdiction and you can apply to it for maintenance. All the details are set out in Chapter 6.

Children Act application

You can apply under the Children Act 1989 for financial orders for the children of the family at any time. If you think that you are going to be filing divorce proceedings reasonably soon, within a year say, then it is probably not a good idea to start Children Act proceedings as it will simply duplicate the financial proceedings under the divorce and add to the cost.

Financial applications and domestic abuse

If you need to get an injunction to protect yourself from abuse is possible to ask the court to make an order to cover payment of outgoings – like rent or mortgage payments – at the same time as it makes an occupation order (see Chapter 8). This short-circuits the previous necessity of having to make a separate application to the court for financial support to cover basic running costs for the home.

Getting legal advice

While a do-it-yourself divorce can be relatively straightforward if you and your spouse/cp can reach an amicable agreement, you will almost certainly need a solicitor's help if this is impossible. If nothing else, this should prevent you giving up any rights that you have because you do not understand the law.

What a solicitor can do for you

If there are going to be questions about dividing property or sorting out arrangements for the children, it is a good idea to have at least one meeting with a solicitor so that you can get some early advice. This may prevent matters from becoming complicated, or one of you getting less than his or her entitlement, and can generally help to take the heat out of the situation.

If you can sort out your financial affairs as equal partners, between yourselves or with the help of a mediator (see Chapter 4), so much the better. Even then, it is still wise for you both to ask a solicitor whether the arrangements seem fair, and to ensure that they are framed in a watertight manner so as not to leave you open for future unexpected financial claims, and so that they do not result in any unnecessary payments of tax.

If you are intending to use mediation as the primary means of sorting out your arrangements comprehensively, ask your solicitor about his or her attitude towards mediation. Some solicitors have now been trained as mediators themselves and are likely to have a more constructive approach towards agreements worked out through mediation, as long as they do not work against your (and the family's) best interests. There are, however, a few, perhaps more old-

fashioned, solicitors who may be instinctively anti-mediation and they may not be helpful in advising you objectively if you do reach arrangements in this way.

DECIDE WHAT'S BEST

A solicitor can be of great help, but try to use his or her services efficiently and economically. Ask yourself whether you want to obtain legal advice or want someone to 'fight' for you. Wanting a solicitor to

Using a solicitor
If it is not possible for the two of you to achieve a fair agreement on your own or using a mediator, a solicitor can negotiate on your behalf. It is not usually possible for you and your spouse/partner to instruct the same solicitor as there is a potential conflict of interest between you.

act for you in a contentious way will involve you in expense which may be out of proportion to anything gained. It is also not at all cost-effective to use a solicitor as an emotional support, whatever the temptations.

Time and money are invariably interlinked. The more you use a solicitor's services, the greater the hole that will be cut into your family finances. What a solicitor can effectively do for you is explained in detail in this chapter. It is of the utmost importance that you consider the question of costs before launching into a major battle. Spending an hour or so (at the very least) with an experienced and competent solicitor to get advice on your legal position is likely to be a worthwhile investment. Of course, how much you want to (or are forced to) involve your solicitor may be constrained by how much you can afford to pay. Explanations and warnings about the problem of costs have already been given. If you have not already done so, read Chapter 1 now.

HANDLING YOUR DIVORCE

It is possible to handle an undefended divorce yourself without a solicitor, although it is probably fair to say that it is at least as hard

> **❝ If your partner flatly refuses to cooperate in any way, or you receive a divorce petition, a solicitor's advice would certainly be useful. ❞**

as doing your own conveyancing on your house (and the financial pitfalls can be worse if something goes wrong). Do-it-yourself divorce packs are widely available but the packs may contain out-of-date forms, so you should double check these with the court. Be wary of taking important steps without legal advice: the packs can give you general but not individual advice, which can be provided only by solicitors or Citizens Advice Bureaux (CABx).

Be particularly wary of the common assumption that getting a divorce means an end to your financial obligations to your ex. Divorce and money matters are considered quite separately by the courts, and getting a divorce does not mean an automatic end to your money concerns.

Sorting out problems over children

Protracted litigation over the children can be extremely expensive. Also, it is harmful to both to the children and to you, and rarely produces a satisfactory

You can also download forms and information leaflets from www.courtservice.gov.uk
Your local county court can also supply you with copies of these.

result. If you cannot come to an agreement by yourselves or through mediation, see if you can arrange a meeting for both of you and your solicitors. A good solicitor will be able to give you sensible advice about the way in which you should deal with the arrangements for the children, and about the attitude that a court would take if you felt that you had to resolve a dispute by going to court. Disputes over children cannot be 'won' or 'lost', and ultimately you are likely to prefer a solution that you reach yourselves, rather than have to accept one imposed upon you by a judge who, however wise and well meaning, does not – and cannot – know you or your children.

Getting a court order for maintenance and division of property

A solicitor will know the appropriate court for the particular order you need and the procedure for applying. He or she will be able to advise you on the attitude that the court will take and your prospects of success.

Getting information about finances

You may find that you are faced with a long, uphill battle to get financial information out of your spouse/cp. However reasonable you want to be over things, and whatever you do, he or she may refuse to disclose assets.

Withholding information at the early stages of financial negotiations does nothing but run up costs and reduce the amount that there is to go round. If you go to see a solicitor, your spouse/partner may then do so too, and may be persuaded to come clean about details of his or her financial situation. You will both need to disclose your finances fully to each other before a proper agreement can be reached.

Sorting out cohabitation problems

Although these fall generally within the scope of family law, not all solicitors have much experience or knowledge about the law as it relates to cohabiting couples. If you have an argument about the ownership or entitlement to the home, you need to find a solicitor who does know about this area of law and understands the trust and property law involved.

Getting an agreement about finances

Good solicitors will impress upon both of you the advantages of cooperation and will help you to negotiate an agreement about finances.

If your resources leave very limited room for manoeuvre, fighting it out in court may not be worthwhile. It is pointless getting your solicitor to try to push for more, or less, if the cost of getting it is going to be more than the amount you are asking for. If

Other solicitor's services

A solicitor can also:

- Put an agreement into wording that is clear and will be acceptable to the court.
- Arrange maintenance and the division of property in a more tax-efficient way.
- Draw up a 'clean-break' settlement where appropriate (particularly where there are no young children).
- Point out things that you may not have thought of: for example, that a one of you may be losing substantial widow(er)'s pension rights under the other's pension scheme.
- Explain how the pension law works.
- Take into account the effects of any proposed order on welfare benefits entitlements.

“Formalizing an agreement need not jeopardize amicable relations with your spouse/partner: indeed, doing so could pave the way for a less painful split.”

money disputes go on for months or years, the costs will run into thousands of pounds even where small amounts are in dispute. Even if you are in receipt of legal aid and do not initially have to pay your solicitor's charges as they arise, you have to do so ultimately under the 'statutory charge' (see Chapter 1).

If you have reached an agreement with your spouse/partner and the issues seem fairly clear cut, it may still be worthwhile considering having one interview with a solicitor to check over the terms of that proposed agreement, particularly if you have reached agreement only about the broad outlines of how you are going to split your finances. Sadly, agreements, especially unwritten, have a habit of unravelling over time unless all their consequences are thought through and the agreements recorded officially.

A note of warning is relevant at this point. Sometimes couples go to their solicitors with an agreement that they have worked out, and are disappointed when the solicitors – very properly – point out the pitfalls concealed within the agreement as it stands. They then blame the solicitors for 'messing things up'. This is to misunderstand the solicitor's role. Solicitors are trained, and paid, to look for the flaws in agreements and attempt to make them watertight. If you have worked out an agreement without first taking legal advice, you may find that you have not taken into account all the long-term legal and practical implications for the future. If your solicitor points them out, he or she is not being unreasonably perverse, but is doing a proper job.

The right solicitor

Before you embark on the search for a solicitor, it is worth considering what he or she can and cannot do for you, and keeping in mind the criteria that you are going to use to help you make your choice. It may be easiest first to define what your solicitor should not be.

Not a hired gun

A solicitor is not (or should not be used as) a hired gun. He or she should be prepared to give you balanced, practical advice, not simply tell you what you want to hear. It is possible that in certain matters you are not right, and your solicitor should retain a degree of professional detachment in your relationship such that he or she can point your error out to you, fairly and sympathetically.

Not a counsellor

A solicitor will give you advice, but he or she is not your counsellor, in the sense of being a therapist. Good solicitors will inevitably have acquired some counselling skills, or even have some counselling training, but that is not their primary function when they are dealing with your split. If you need counselling or therapy, you should go to someone who is properly qualified to provide this for you, in a therapeutic environment. Using your solicitor in this way will prove dreadfully expensive and will interfere with what he or she needs to do for you. Your solicitor may well suggest that counselling might help, and may even be able to recommend someone who is skilled in dealing with the area of family breakdown.

Not a friend

Your solicitor is not your friend, though a good solicitor will have a friendly manner and be kind and sympathetic. But resist the temptation to be too intimate in your relationship. There needs to be a certain amount of professional detachment between the two of you, for your good as much as for the solicitor's. Pushing the relationship to friendship will probably result in longer conversations – and greater expense for you. If you have a friend who is a solicitor it may be possible to instruct him or her, but you may find that such a friend would prefer not to act for you even though he or she will offer you supportive general advice.

WHAT TO LOOK FOR IN A SOLICITOR

What people want in a solicitor varies tremendously – a solicitor who is perfect for one client may not be ideal for another. Before you start looking for one, it is worth thinking about the sort of person that you would like to act for you. You may have certain personal preferences: would you, for example, feel more comfortable with a solicitor of the same gender as you? Would you like him or her to be older than you? Do you want to be steered by your solicitor or do you want to 'direct' him or her? Clearly, the qualities, both professional and personal, of the solicitor are crucial.

The following factors are indicators of a good solicitor:

- **Intelligence and thoughtfulness** are probably more crucial than experience. A good family solicitor will be inclined to approach your difficulties with your ex in a constructive way, exploring whether an amicable solution can be achieved. But this does not mean he or she should be a pushover – your solicitor should be prepared to be tough on your behalf if need be. Be wary, however, of any solicitor who talks in swaggering terms (for example, 'We'll take your husband for every penny he owns'). However hell-bent you are on revenge, you must bear in mind that an overly aggressive approach is going to be enormously expensive and, very often, counterproductive.

- **Organization and efficiency.** Look at the way in which the solicitor's firm presents itself – is the phone answered promptly? Does the secretary seem sensible, and does he or she take down a proper message? Are your calls returned as promised? Do you know who will take a phone call if the solicitor is not in the office?

- **Their office environment.** Solicitors' offices are busy places to work, but if they are downright dirty and depressing and nobody has made any effort to make the waiting room a reasonable place to sit in, it can speak volumes about the firm's attitude to its clients.

- **Good communication.** Does the solicitor treat you like a human being, or as just a problem to be processed? Are you listened to politely and carefully? Does he or she behave in a professional manner? For example, other clients' paperwork should not be left out where you can see it.

If you are not happy with your solicitor it is probably best to change to another one early on in the case. Even if you are legally aided you can still change solicitors, but you would need to explain to the Legal Services Commission (LSC) why you were not happy and why you needed to change, and get the transfer of the certificate agreed.

❝ It helps if he or she is experienced in family law, but this is not crucial in a team or department setting where there are experienced staff to turn to if the need arises. **❞**

 Unprofessional behaviour
You should not have to put up with unprofessional behaviour from your solicitor. When you are feeling unhappy because of your family situation, it is easy to feel that you just have to take what you find, particularly if you are legally aided. However, this is absolutely not the case and you should not have to accept unprofessional conduct of any kind.

FINDING A SOLICITOR

It may be that a solicitor you have used in the past for some other matter (for example, buying a house) does family work or has a colleague who does. It might be worth asking and having a preliminary discussion on the telephone. However, if he or she has previously acted for both you and your spouse/partner, professional rules say that he or she may not be able to act for you (or your spouse/partner) because of the potential for 'conflict of interest'.

Ask acquaintances who have been through a family split whom they used, although you should be wary of recommendations in cases which are very different from your own. It is also worthwhile making enquiries at your local CAB or advice centre or even your local county court (each court keeps a list of solicitors who appear before the court). The Law Society's Regional Directories of solicitors practising in the area and showing the categories of the work they undertake are available in CABx, public libraries and court offices throughout the UK. The Directories and CABx should also be able to point you in the direction of lawyers who have LSC contracts.

Resolution (which used to be called the Solicitors Family Law Association) is in practice a very good source for tracking down a specialist family lawyer. It is an association of over 5,000 matrimonial lawyers in England and Wales who must subscribe to a code of practice (which you can

 Finding a solicitor: Community Legal Service: 0845 345 4345. www.clsdirect.org.uk
Law Society: 0870 606 2555 www.lawsociety.org.uk
Resolution: 01689 820272 www.resolution.org.uk

read on their website) designed to encourage and assist parties to reach acceptable arrangements for the future in a positive and conciliatory – rather than in an aggressive and litigious – way. This does not mean that a Resolution solicitor will be 'soft'. His or her advice to you and manner of dealing with the various issues that arise will be positive.

You can also ask the administrative secretary of Resolution for a list of the solicitor members in your region, or search the Resolution directory on its website. If there are no Resolution solicitors practising in your area, you can use the website or telephone the Records Section of the Law Society of England and Wales.

The task of finding a solicitor through Yellow Pages and its electronic version, www.yell.co.uk is relatively easy because in most directories there are special sections for solicitors who are members of Resolution, identified by its logo, as well as for solicitors who offer legal aid. Look under the heading 'Solicitors' (usually there is very little listed under 'Divorce').

When you telephone or write to a firm of solicitors asking for an appointment, say that you wish to be advised in connection with your matrimonial difficulties and ask whether the firm has a solicitor who specialises in family matters, preferably one who is a member of Resolution. If you have been cohabiting, you should check the solicitor's experience in this field.

Accreditation schemes

Both the Law Society and Resolution have accreditation schemes for family lawyers. To be a member of the Resolution scheme a person has to:

- Have been a solicitor for at least five years (or a Fellow of the Institute of Legal Executives, a professional body representing over 22,000 legal executives and trainee legal executives – see Lawyers who are not solicitors. box – for the same period).

Lawyers who are not solicitors

There are many experienced matrimonial lawyers employed by solicitors' firms who are not qualified solicitors. Previously called 'managing clerks', they are now known as 'legal executives'. Many are Fellows of the Institute of Legal Executives or are working towards qualification as Fellows. (Traditionally they came into the profession straight from school and learnt on the job. Increasingly these days, they have degree-level education.) They are likely to be just as competent as the solicitors whom they work with, and the same considerations apply to them as to solicitors when you are finding someone suitable to act for you.

- Pass a special examination.
- Have worked at least half of his or her working hours over the past three years as a family lawyer.
- Subscribe to the code of practice. The Law Society's Family Law Panel has different standards: solicitors or legal executives have to have been qualified for three years and should have worked as family lawyers for one-third of the total of practice time for the past three years.

 The Bar Council's Pro-Bono Unit is a scheme whereby barristers (or counsel) offer free legal advice to deserving cases: 020 7611 9500 www.barprobono.org.uk
Eail: enquiries@barprobono.org.uk

Getting the best out of your solicitor

Try to use your solicitor's time as efficiently as possible. A succinct letter to him or her setting out what you want to do (your 'instructions') may well be more cost-effective than a long, rambling telephone conversation.

If you can go prepared for your first interview, so much the better. Some solicitors send a questionnaire to their clients to be completed and returned before the first interview.

Documents to take with you to your first solicitor's appointment

- Your marriage/cp certificate (if you are married).
- Any correspondence or assessments from the Child Support Agency.
- Copies of any court orders made about your marriage – or about your children.
- Typed or neatly written notes setting out:
  - your name in full, and those of your spouse/partner and children
  - dates of birth of yourself, your spouse/partner and children
  - details of any children in the household who are not children of you both
  - your address and (if different) that of your spouse/partner
  - your home and work telephone numbers (and your email address if you have one)
  - your occupation and that of your spouse/partner
  - your National Insurance number (for legal aid applications)
  - names and addresses of the children's schools
  - dates of any previous marriage of yourself and/or your spouse/partner and dates of any final decrees
  - if you have already separated, the date and circumstances of the separation.
- A summary of your financial position (see Chapter 2).
- Any correspondence that you might have received from your spouse/partner's solicitor.

It may help to go prepared with notes of what you want to ask and then to take notes of the advice given. Indeed, this is a sensible precaution as otherwise it is all too easy to forget everything your solicitor has told you.

Remember that you can accept or reject advice as you wish. But before you reject advice, make sure that you understand the point.

Using your solicitor's time wisely and cost-effectively means not leaving it to your solicitor to do everything: because of the time basis of costing the bill, the more time he or she spends on the case, the higher the bill will be. Quite a lot can be done by you yourself that will save costs, but you need to tell your solicitor first what you plan to do.

Open your own file at home and be organised about keeping correspondence and any relevant documents safe, and keep copies of letters that you send to your solicitor.

You are entitled to be told at any stage how the case is progressing and how much it is costing. Your solicitor should send you a client care letter (see below) at the outset. Remember that you can ask him or her for interim statements of how costs are building up if they

❝ To use your solicitor to the best advantage, do not hesitate at any time to ask him or her to explain and discuss any points about which you are not clear. ❞

Low-priced interviews
Although it can be tempting to forget about the question of costs, this is an area which you ignore at your peril. Running up hefty legal bills, whether you are paying privately or have public funding, will severely damage the ability of both partners to begin their lives afresh. Costs are dealt with at length in Chapter 1.

are not supplied automatically (firms should do this).

Client care code

All solicitors must comply with a client care code, which sets out how clients should be kept informed and advised on who will be handling their case and about costs.

Family Law Protocol: www.lawsociety.org.uk follow the links to 'products and services' and then 'publications and gifts' to download it from the Law Society's website, or buy it from the Law Society if you wish.

What this means in practice is that at the outset of your case – once you have seen and informed a solicitor that you want him or her to take on your case – you should receive a fairly detailed letter (sometimes called a 'client care' letter) which complies with the code. This might tell you, for example, the name of the person dealing with your case, the name of the head of the department and information about costs. It should also identify the person to complain to in the firm if you think you have got poor service. If your solicitor does not send out such a letter, it may be an indication that he or she is not really on the ball – so you may get better service elsewhere.

The Family Law Protocol

Family law solicitors should all conform to the tenets of good practice set out in the Family Law Protocol, which is a code published by the Law Society and devised by it in conjunction with the Solicitors Family Law Society, the Legal Services Commission and the Lord Chancellor's Department.

The conduct it sets out is not mandatory but advisory. However, if a solicitor does not observe the rules of practice that it sets out, he or she

could run the risk of costs orders being made against him or her.

COMPLAINTS ABOUT SOLICITORS

Occasionally the relationship between a client and a solicitor can break down. If you have a grievance against your solicitor (for example, if he or she persistently fails to return your telephone calls or to respond to your letters), it may be worthwhile having a word with the person identified in the client care letter as the one to complain to. You could also try talking to the head of the family law department or otherwise the senior partner of the firm (the name on the top of the notepaper).

Switching to another solicitor can be an expensive process, as the new person will have to read through all the paperwork that has already been produced: this can itself cause extra delay. So, if a sincere personal intervention can restore a good working relationship with your solicitor, this often is the best action to take.

If, however, the situation fails to improve, you may wish to complain formally about your solicitor. Complaints are handled by the

Law Society Consumer Complaints Service: Victoria Court, 8 Dormer Place, Leamington Spa, CV32 5AE. 0845 608 6565. General enquiries: 01926 820082 www.legalcomplaints.org.uk

Consumer Complaints Service of the Law Society.

Complaints about barristers

Another possibility is that you may have a complaint against your barrister or counsel, if one is instructed by your solicitor to act on your behalf – say, at a court hearing. Complaints about barristers can be hard to succeed with, but it is a good idea to check with your solicitor first to see if your grounds for grievance are well founded. Complaints about barristers should be made to the Bar Council.

TAKING A COMPLAINT FURTHER

Once your complaint against a solicitor or a barrister has been investigated, the next stage, if you are still unhappy, is to write to the Legal Services Ombudsman. She oversees the handling of complaints against solicitors, barristers and licensed conveyancers.

OTHER SOURCES OF ADVICE AND HELP

Anyone in difficulties over finance, tax, housing, the children, or rights generally, can go for advice to a Citizens Advice Bureau (CAB). All CABx have numerous leaflets and information about local sources of help and services. Their services differ across the UK, but many can provide you with everything from an impartial listener to representation at social security appeal tribunals or advice about money and county court representation. CABx are especially good at providing debt-counselling services. You can find the address of your local branch in the telephone directory.

 The Bar Council: 289-293 High Holborn, London WC1V 7HZ. www.barcouncil.org.uk
Office of the Legal Services Ombudsman: Sunlight House, Quay Street, Manchester M3 3JZ.
www.olso.org

Using the internet

As the many 'go further' boxes throughout the text indicate, the internet is now an easy source of information. Family law is no exception. But you should bear in mind that the information on the internet is not monitored for accuracy: you must be sure only to rely on information from reliable, official sites. Even then, it is important to check the date when information was posted, to make sure that it is up to date.

USING THE INTERNET TO FIND A SOLICITOR

Given the increasing use of the internet as a source of information, you may wish to find a solicitor this way. The usefulness of the internet in this area is still somewhat limited, but improving all the time. Family lawyers are increasingly using the internet as a means of contacting potential clients by creating their own websites, but there are some exceptions. Your chances of success in finding a local solicitor on the internet are closely linked to where you are – London and other major cities are generally better served. The easiest way is to go via the websites listed on page 66. You can use search engines and use particular keywords – 'divorce', 'family lawyer', 'family mediation' – ensuring that your search is limited to the UK. You could also type in your locality (for example,

Manchester) and see what comes up. Many legal websites are somewhat 'boring' but at least they should give you an idea of what is on offer at a firm. Other sites will include full explanations of their services and fees, pictures of solicitors (so you can see what they look like) and sometimes 'update' pages which you can visit to get free information.

ONLINE LEGAL ADVICE

It is important to weigh up the likely bias of any website that you go to, as this may distort the information that it supplies.

❝It's always worth looking at a number of websites and comparing information so that you get a broad view of your position. ❞

73

Websites tend to fall into one of three categories:

- Government or government-funded sites: these will be dedicated to providing quality impartial advice. Generally they will be kept up-to-date.
- Reputable charities and advice organisations: these also tend to be a good source of accurate information. The larger and more well-established the organisation, the better the advice is likely to be. Some will have a particular bias in terms of their focus: advice for gay and lesbian couples, or for lone parents, for instance.
- Pressure and special interest groups and private websites: you may have to be more careful with these. They may have sprung from particular grievances or problems with the legal system. The legal advice that they offer may be distorted by this and, because they may not be very well funded, they may not have the resources to keep the information on the site up to date.

❝You should know that getting your divorce via the internet will not make it any quicker than it would otherwise be, and the court fee will not be cheaper. The court procedure remains the same.❞

Online divorces

There are internet services that offer you a divorce package. They will supply you with divorce forms (for a fee) and (for a further fee) help you to fill them in. However, if you do want to do your own divorce, you can get the forms and guidance free from the Court Service website www.courtservice.gov.uk and complete them yourself. It is probably not a very good idea to do this unless your marriage has been fairly short, you have no children and you are entirely amicable about how you are going to divide up the family assets.

Mediation and collaborative law

Couples facing family break-up have a wide choice of services to help them get through the situation. This chapter deals with mediation: how separating couples can get skilled help to sort out their disputes over the split and all the issues involved – money, the home, businesses, debts, pensions, and not least the children – without building up unbearably heavy legal costs.

4

Family mediation

Family mediation has been developing in the USA since the 1960s and emerged in the UK in 1977: it was first used in the UK in relation to disputes involving children in Bristol County Court. Since then it has grown to become a voluntary process encompassing all issues which arise in the wake of family breakdown.

WHAT IS MEDIATION?

Defining mediation is not easy. Dictionary definitions of the word do not capture the complex nature of mediation as practised in family matters. The two definitions shown in the boxes opposite were drafted in days before mediators dealt widely with the breakup of cohabiting relationships, so they may sound as though they only deal with married couples. This is not the case; increasingly mediators deal with all sorts of family relationships.

Mediation is becoming more and more popular. 2006 saw the launch of the Family Mediation Helpline, part of a government initiative to encourage as many as possible of us to consider mediation as a way of resolving family disputes.

Ideally, mediation should be a process that neither party feels constrained to go in for – compulsion would ruin the rationale for mediation. The insistence that those obtaining legal aid – see Chapter 1 – have to explore the idea of mediation seems to fly in the face of this. Fortunately, mediation services which offer these appointments are conscious of this and are sensitive to the feelings of people who feel unwilling to go through the procedure.

Definition of mediation

Mediation defined in The Code of Practice for Family Mediators produced by National Family Mediation (NFM) and the Family Mediators Association (FMA):

'...a process in which an impartial third person assists those involved in family breakdown, and in particular separating or divorcing couples, to communicate better with one another and to reach their own agreed and informed decisions about some or all of the issues relating to, or arising from, the separation, divorce, children, finance or property'.

CONFIDENTIALITY

Mediation is 'legally privileged', which means that nothing said in the context of the sessions can be used in evidence at court if, eventually, legal action through the courts has to be taken. Also, any wish not to disclose an address to the partner will be respected. Documents disclosing financial information during mediation are, however, usually treated as 'open', which means that they could be disclosed as evidence if there is a court case over money issues later on.

However, there are two important exceptions to both the confidentiality and privilege attached to mediation:

- where someone, particularly a child, appears to be suffering or is likely to suffer 'significant harm' (for example, sexual abuse), the mediator may have to stop the mediation process and take steps to protect the child. What steps will be taken in practice may very often form part of the discussion between the mediator and the couple.
- where the mediator is under a legal duty to make disclosure to the appropriate government authorities under the Proceeds of Crime Act 2002 and/or the

Definition of mediation

Mediation defined in Resolution's Family Mediation Code of Practice:

1.1 a couple or any family members
1.2 whether or not they are legally represented
1.3 and at any time, whether or not there have been legal proceedings
1.4 agree to the appointment of a neutral third party (the mediator)
1.5 who is impartial
1.6 who has no authority to make any decisions with regard to their issues
1.7 which may relate to separation, divorce, children's issues, property and financial questions or any other issues that may raise
1.8 but who helps them reach their own informed decisions
1.9 by negotiated agreement
1.10 without adjudication.

66 Mediation can take place at any time, even before legal proceedings have been started. **99**

relevant money laundering regulations. This would occur if either of you revealed that you had finances that you had acquired as the result of some criminal activity (this includes benefit or tax fraud). In such circumstances the mediator would have to end the mediation with you.

TYPES OF MEDIATION

If you opt for mediation, you will need to decide whether to choose a family mediator with a therapeutic or mental-health background (a 'family mediator') or one with a legal background (a 'lawyer mediator').

The former are, generally, mediators who have a background in social work or mental health (like therapists, counsellors, family court welfare officers, or social workers) and are therefore experienced in family problems. The latter are mediators who are experienced family lawyers; their particular skill and expertize is knowing what the law is with regard to family matters and how the courts are likely to deal with cases. Some services offer co-mediation (see below), where a family mediator and lawyer mediator work together. You should check what experience a mediator has before going to him or her. Advice on how to find a mediator is given later in this chapter.

Jargon buster

Conciliation Interchangeable with mediation, though sometimes used to indicate that it is taking place in court, rather than entirely voluntarily. Not to be confused with reconciliation.

AIM or 'all issues mediation' Mediation over finances and any issues about the children.

Child only mediation Mediation only concerned with issues about the children such as residence and contact.

Lawyer mediator A mediator who is also a qualified lawyer, but who will not take a lawyer's role in the mediation.

Family mediator A mediator who is not a lawyer but will have come from some other background, often social work, teaching or counselling.

Family mediators

These have historically been cheaper than lawyer mediators (for more details on how much mediation costs, see the end of this chapter). Some family mediation services charge fees based on a couple's income or even offer free sessions.

Lawyer mediators

Because lawyer mediators offer more by way of legal information than family mediators do, it is more meaningful to compare their costs with those incurred by each spouse instructing a solicitor and both solicitors running up heavy costs. Thus a husband and wife can potentially, by using a lawyer mediator rather than a solicitor, cut their legal costs considerably.

There are advantages in having a skilled lawyer assisting in the mediation process: although lawyer mediators do not advise either party individually, they draw on their own experience of family-law cases in first of all piecing together an accurate picture of the family's finances, and then in helping the couple work out realistic (and legally acceptable) solutions. Although mediators cannot offer advice, they can give the couple correct, up-to-date information on the rapidly changing law – such as changes in the law on pensions and child support, and in procedure – so their clients can make well-informed choices during mediation. Family mediators often have an arrangement with a local solicitor who will check over the terms of an agreement towards the end of the mediation, but this may be rather late in the day to correct any wrong turnings made in the mediation process. However, an increasing number of NFM services are now using lawyer mediators too, so check with your local service.

Lawyer mediators will almost certainly charge more than family mediators, although some operate discretionary lower rates for low income families.

Benefits of mediation
Each spouse should still get independent legal advice, but because a couple may well reach an agreement more quickly through a mediator than through separate solicitors, cost savings can be achieved.

Co-mediation

The type of mediation service where a pair of mediators - a family mediator and a lawyer mediator - work together, known as co-mediation, was pioneered by the FMA, and is now used in many NFM services as well.

The mediation process

Most mediation services start by offering you a short meeting so that they can explain to you how mediation works and check whether mediation would be suitable for you.

THE FIRST SESSION

If you qualify for legal aid this is worked out and you complete the forms at this meeting. This is sometimes called an 'intake meeting'. Some services offer joint intake meetings that you both attend, others generally see you each separately. These meetings give you each the chance to decide whether you want to go ahead. If you both want to go ahead, and the mediator thinks it will be suitable for you both, then you will be invited to the first mediation session. This will probably last for one to two hours. Most services will arrange this so that you are both in the same room with the mediator, but sometimes it may be better for you to be in separate

rooms and for the mediator to go between you. This is called 'shuttle mediation'.

For mediation to work, both of you need to attend. It can be a daunting prospect to face your ex in the same room to discuss what future arrangements should be made, but a skilled mediator, who will always be impartial, will help by managing the process so that both parties can make their views clear. It is the mediator's responsibility to be even-handed, to create a balance between the parties so that they can both negotiate properly over conflicts. Even where you feel very much in conflict with one another, addressing conflict is common in mediation and the right solutions can often be found. Mediation is very often the most appropriate forum for conflicts to be resolved.

66 If you are afraid of your partner, or do not want to see him or her, tell the mediation service. They should be able to make sure that you feel safe and offer separate waiting and meeting rooms. **99**

A POSITIVE APPROACH

A mediator will not impose his or her own views, but will try to help you find common ground so that together you can craft arrangements which will work for each of you individually and the family as a whole. Sometimes this process can mean that a mediator will encourage the more passive partner to put his or her own views forward and ensure that the more dominant partner stays quieter.

The agreement to mediate forms the basis of the terms on which a mediator will act in a mediation, and will therefore set out what you agree to in the mediation.

❝ At the first session the mediator will explain what the process of mediation is all about and the terms of the mediation agreement. ❞

HOW IT WORKS

Mediation works by setting agendas covering the issues each of you wants to discuss – it is up to you both to decide what you need to talk about. The agenda for the first session could cover, for example, the decision to separate, arrangements for the time being over the children, and payment of bills. The process of mediation can take about five to six sessions, although more or fewer may be necessary. Mediations are usually

❝ The mediator will establish ground rules to create a more positive framework for working things out. ❞

relatively informal, with first names being used if you wish.

As part and parcel of the agreement, in all-issues mediation you must both consent to give full disclosure of your finances.

Each of you may be expected to fill out a comprehensive form giving details about your income including:
- savings
- debts
- pensions
- the home
- family
- income from a business

You will have to supply back-up documents if need be. The forms are then sent to the mediator (usually by at least the third session), with a copy for the other partner. If you have already compiled the financial dossier in Chapter 2 you will find that this is an easier task.

To ensure that both of you are fully aware of the whole picture of the family's finances, the mediator will often put up the figures on a flipchart. Getting things up on a chart in this way helps identify any areas where more information is needed and clarify which money matters are issues between you. The lengthy (and costly) process of 'disclosure' in court cases is short-circuited by this method, because one of you can often quickly identify if the other is holding back information and ensure that the figures are corrected. Often, various alternative arrangements or options are written up on the flipchart. Each of you can put forward your own options. If either of you gets stuck, the mediator can help out, so more creative solutions to vexed problems can be worked through and tested as to how well they will work in reality.

MEMORANDUM OF UNDERSTANDING

As and when an agreement is reached, the mediator will prepare a summary of the agreement for each of you and your solicitors. This is generally called a 'Memorandum of Understanding'. The mediator will also prepare an 'open' summary of information about money matters,

❝ If you reach a financial agreement this must be put into a court order or a legally binding form such as a 'deed' setting out the agreement. You will generally need a solicitor to do this for you. ❞

but any agreement reached is 'without prejudice' – that is, it cannot be made known to the court at a full hearing if the agreement subsequently breaks down. The agreement can then be translated by the solicitors into court documents – the divorce and a consent order over finances, for example.

Having your own solicitor also means you have legal back-up in case any urgent legal action needs to be taken – to prevent your spouse/cp from disposing of assets, for example – or if the mediation does not result in an agreement (in which case you will probably still

Are solicitors still necessary?

Even if you have gone in for mediation, it is still a good idea for you individually to get legal advice about what rights and responsibilities you have (so that you can negotiate on an informed basis) and also to double-check the terms of any agreement made during mediation. You can check whether the agreement will be watertight, whether anything has been missed out and whether you are giving away something you should not.

have to go to court or your solicitors may be able to negotiate on your behalf). Thus legal advice is complementary to the mediation process. But by using a skilled and knowledgeable mediator, you could save thousands of pounds in legal fees by avoiding a full-blown legal battle.

MEDIATION AND THE CHILDREN

Mediation takes a family-based approach, rather than the adversarial approach adopted in the family courts, where parents have to be on opposite sides, which is a distinct drawback when it comes to dealing with the children. You need to try to work together to sort out how the children will be looked after when the family separates, and the family-based approach of mediation can often help you cooperate as parents in planning for your children's and your own futures.

It problems over arrangements for the children are just a part of broader difficulties over finance generally, mediation involving a lawyer mediator would be a better bet. Try to ensure that, if possible, comprehensive, or 'all-issues', mediation is available.

" If the dispute is only over the children, mediation by a family mediator may well be the best option. "

The emphasis in mediation is on enabling you to create solutions which enable you to remain parents in as full a sense as possible. By meeting in a neutral environment in the presence of a non-partisan, experienced professional (or sometimes two professionals) trained in assisting couples to come to realistic agreements, you both may find that you can at least (and perhaps at last) communicate directly rather than talking at each other or entirely missing each other's points. With your agreement, the children themselves may occasionally be invited to the mediation, but they should only attend if being there helps them cope with the family split.

The UK College of Family Mediators: www.ukcfm.co.uk or look in Yellow Pages under 'Mediation' (www.yell.com)
Relate : 01788 573241/0845 456 1310 www.relate.org.uk

Is mediation appropriate for you?

The potential benefits of mediation are numerous, but it doesn't necessarily suit every couple or every family situation. This section will give you an outline of the procedure involved.

As a rule of thumb, consider whether you feel that, with expert help, you would be able to negotiate with your spouse/ partner with respect to yourself and him or her. If you feel you would either give in too easily, or try to dominate the process and refuse to listen, then mediation may not be right for you.

FREE MEDIATION WITH LEGAL AID

As Chapter 1 made clear, if you qualify for legal aid for Help with Mediation, you will get funding for your mediation and subsequent advice from a solicitor without making a financial contribution and, crucially, without incurring the statutory charge (see Chapter 1).

COLLABORATIVE LAW

This process originated in the USA as a way of resolving disputes without going to court. In the last few years it has been taught and practised in this country, and there are increasing numbers of lawyers across the country who have learned the techniques and offer it as a service to their clients.

What does mediation cost?

The more sessions you have, the more mediation will cost. Three to six sessions are typical where there are a number of issues to resolve; fewer sessions are likely if the dispute involves a single issue. It is impossible to give detailed guidelines on fees as these will vary from service to service. Fees will generally be charged by the hour, and many services will operate a sliding scale of contribution based on your income. Each of you will be separately assessed and charged. Expect to pay for each session as it takes place.

❝ Of couples sent to explore the possibility of mediation for legal aid, between 20 and 30 per cent go on to mediation. **❞**

Advantages of mediation

- **Control over the outcome** Together you create your own, tailor-made solutions to problems involved in the family split – arrangements which will suit your family, not ones imposed on you by the courts. Solutions worked out in mediation can indeed cover aspects where the court would have no power to make court orders.

- **Speed and cost-effectiveness** The process is speedier – disputes can be resolved in weeks, not months and years – and more cost-effective. Costs are likely to be measured in at most hundreds, not thousands, of pounds; you may even get free mediation with legal aid.

- **Respect for the family** Members of the family can come to value others more. The mediation process can help improve communication between you both and aid cooperation over the children. The process of splitting up can be made more dignified.

- **Confidentiality** The whole discussion in mediation is private and confidential. If you want to ensure privacy and confidentiality over how you work things out, mediation may be right for you.

In the collaborative process you both:
- Have lawyers.
- Enter into a binding agreement that you will not go to court.
- Have a duty to give full and frank disclosure of all your financial circumstances.

The process involves a number of meetings at which both clients and lawyers are present, and everyone tries to work towards an agreement. Unlike mediation, during which the mediator can give information but not advice, the lawyers advise their clients during the process. Some of the advice may be given by a lawyer to his or her own client, but advice can also be given and discussed

> **❝ Either of you can choose, at a later stage, to opt out of the process and go to court instead, but you will need a new lawyer to take the case on. ❞**

Family Mediators Association: 0117 946 7062 www.fma.co.uk
Family Mediation Helpline 0845 60 26 627 or see their website: www.familymediationhelpline.co.uk
Or you can use Resolution: www.resolution.org.uk

openly in the meetings. This can avoid some of the frustrating delays in mediation, which occur when people need to consult their lawyers about what they have negotiated. A number of techniques that are used in mediation are also used in the process. The emphasis is very much on helping clients to find solutions that are best for the family as a whole and that will work for the future.

Collaborative law
Collaborative law is not necessarily cheaper, and legal aid is not specifically available to cover the collaborative process so ask for an estimate of costs when you are considering this option.

However the actual time spent dealing with your case will not always be less. What should save costs is your decision not to go to court.

How do I find a collaborative lawyer?

Numbers of trained collaborative lawyers are growing rapidly as training programmes spread the practice. Those who practice it in England at the moment are members of the Collaborative Family Law Organization, which is under the umbrella of Resolution. There is a directory of members on their website.

❝ Your lawyers may also make sure there is a team of other people available, such as financial advisers and counsellors, so that their clients can have the benefit of these skills as well. **❞**

How much does it cost?

Lawyers will charge their normal hourly rates and the work that they will do is very labour intensive because of the meetings. A case may well resolve in a shorter length of time because the delays that correspondence causes will be reduced, and this may save costs.

Collaborative Family Law Organization
www.collablaw.org.uk PO Box 302, Orpington, Kent BR6 8QX Tel: 01689 820272

Divorce and children

If you, as an individual or as a couple, are thinking about splitting up and you have children, you need to think carefully about how you tell them and what plans you make for their future. This chapter offers some general pointers about sensible ways of handling the situation. It also explains the legal side of things, and what happens if you can't agree.

Preparing the children

It is important to acknowledge that you are not going to be at your best as parents during the split and the legal processes. You are likely to be unhappy and stressed and this is going to make it difficult for you to be rational and even-tempered.

You probably feel that you need looking after yourself, and that could result in feelings of guilt, making it harder for you to be the good parent that you would like to be.

Try to take comfort from the fact that this is only temporary. Things will change, even though it may take time. A year from now, life should be different - very probably better - but you need to get through a bad patch as a family, each looking after one another.

You may stop living together, but you will still be the children's parents. They are not going to stop being your children when they reach 18; they will still need you there for weddings, births, illnesses and crises. Do you both really want to be in a state of armed truce every time you meet? Do you want your

children to feel that they can never invite both of you to the same occasion? Do you want to continue to hate each other for the rest of your lives? Somehow you need to find a way of coping with each other in the future.

MAKING A PARENTING PLAN

It is helpful to think about your role as parents over the longer term as well as in the immediate future. You may find it useful to create a 'parenting plan' in which you write down any thoughts and discuss them as a couple.

The Department for Constitutional Affairs (DCA) has produced some excellent leaflets for parents and children - available in several languages - which you can download from the DCA website or obtain from solicitors, mediation services and CABx. The leaflets are aimed at children of different ages, and the parents' leaflet offers advice that you can use when discussing, and deciding, issues about the children's future. They also cover aspects of children's lives that you

“However much your relationship with your spouse or partner has changed, remember that you are both going to go on being parents for the rest of your lives. ”

might not consider immediately, but which could cause difficulties in the future.

TELLING THE CHILDREN

All the experts advise that, if possible, you and your spouse/partner should tell the children about your separation or divorce together, and you should ensure that the children can ask questions and talk, and be hugged and reassured. This may be impossible - if your spouse/partner has left without warning and you are left with the children, you will face their questions alone.

Try not to tell them just before they go to bed, otherwise they may feel abandoned and lie in bed worrying about what will happen.

- Think about what you are going to say. If the two of you can tell the children together, it helps to have worked out what you are going to say beforhand, and to be in a position to tell them about your plans for the future.
- Tell them what the contact arrangements are. If they are old enough, you can discuss these with them, too. It is important, however, that they do not feel that they are being asked to take the responsibility for the decisions.

" Often older children have fairly complicated social lives of their own, so parents need to respect the commitments they already have and factor them in when making plans for the future. "

How the children may feel

Even if your relationship with your spouse/partner has reached the point where you feel that you can no longer carry on living together, and the strains have become all too clear to you, you may well find that the prospect of a separation comes as a shock to the children, and they are likely to react with disbelief, denial and a frantic attempt to make it not happen.

Most children would rather keep their parents together at all costs, even when they know that they are unhappy. Moreover, it is quite common for children to blame themselves for what has happened – they conclude that their father or mother has left because they have been naughty.

When you break the news to them it is important to stress that it is an adult decision, and that though you do not feel that you can go on being

 Family leaflets from the Department for Constitutional Affairs
www.dca.gov.uk/family/divleaf.htm

Part 1: Divorce and children

married you still love them very much and are going to go on being their parents. This is a message that you will have to repeat many times. Tempting as it is, especially if you feel that the problem lies with your spouse/partner, try to keep blame out of it as far as the children are concerned.

> **! Care with terminology**
> It is worth remembering that young children tend to associate words such as 'law' and 'courts' with criminal law and prison so any reference of this kind can be much more alarming than you have anticipated.

Younger children

Younger children may well not understand very much of what is going on, though some may already have come across other children whose parents have split up. You will need to explain the situation in words that they can understand. It is tempting to fudge the issue and not tell the whole truth – say, to suggest that a separation will be for only a little while when you know that it is going to be permanent. It is probably better to be honest at this stage, rather than let the children cling to a false hope that will eventually disappoint them.

Older children

Older children may be used to being consulted about their wishes and could be very clear about which parent they want to live with or preferred contact. Try hard, however, not to let them feel that they are being asked to choose between you and your spouse/partner. It is not fair to burden them with such a choice. Parents should bear in mind that older children may wish to live with one parent for a few years and then change to the other.

Adult children

It is tempting to think that once the children have reached the age of 18 and left home, a divorce will not affect them very much. Many couples preserve a failing marriage until the youngest child has gone to university for this reason. However, young people in their late teens and early twenties can be badly upset by their parents splitting up. It can be particularly hard if their family home disappears while they are away, their bedrooms are no longer as they left them and the neighbourhood that they grew up in is lost.

Try to bear in mind that, although they are adults in the eyes of the law, they are still likely to be dependent on you. It will be better if you can tell them together, and when they are at home. This is preferable to while they are away at college, or right at the end of the holiday, so that they go back to college to face the shock alone.

WHAT YOU CAN DO TO HELP

Tips from parents who have been through it:

66 Tell the schools as soon as you have told the children, or even beforehand. It is bound to affect their school work or behaviour to some extent. If the school knows, staff will be sympathetic and do what they can to help. 99

66 Try to stick to old domestic routines, and stay the same about discipline and behaviour. It would have been very easy to spoil them to make up for hurting them so much. They needed the old routines so they didn't feel the whole world had come smashing down around them. 99

66 You need to talk to the kids a lot, but you have to try not to confide in them in the way that you would in an adult friend. There were times when it was very tempting, but I didn't want to burden them with my side of the story. 99

66 Take advantage of any offer of adult help that you can get. If friends offer to take the children out to let you have a rest, accept gratefully. Life as a single parent is very hard work. It is not an admission of failure to accept help. 99

66 Widen the family circle. It is easy to retreat into your small family world when a divorce hits you. But it can be very claustrophobic and make you more miserable. Instead, try to invite the children's friends home, and get other adults to come round. If you can make your home into an open, friendly place, the children will find it easier to adjust to the new situation. 99

66 Children can be helped by adult friends of their own. And many find it easier to talk with uncles, aunts, godparents or family friends, so try and encourage this. 99

The legal position

The law concerning children is mostly contained in the Children Act 1989 which introduced the concepts of parental responsibility, residence and contact. There are no assumptions that one parent will be better at looking after children than another. There are no legal guidelines about the 'right' amount of contact; what suits one family may not be right for another. The Act puts the needs and welfare of the child first.

PARENTAL RESPONSIBILITY

The Children Act defines parental responsibility as 'all the rights, duties, powers, responsibilities and authority which by law a parent of a child has in relation to the child and his property'. In practice, this means the responsibility and the right to make choices over the issues involved in bringing up a child, like:

- Where the child will live.
- Where the child will go to school.
- What religious upbringing the child will have.
- What medical treatment the child will have.

If you have parental responsibility, you can also apply for a passport for the child.

See the chart for how you get Parental Responsibility. Both parents also get parental responsibility if they adopt a child. Anyone who gets a Residence Order (see page 97) gets Parental Responsibility with it. Parents continue to share this after divorce until the children are 18, whether the children live with them or not.

If you are living together as parents, the law assumes that you will make joint decisions and exercise your parental responsibility together. Once you are separated you can each (in law) exercise that responsibility without consulting the other, but it obviously makes sense to continue to discuss matters, such as those listed above, and to try to reach joint decisions. Sometimes in an emergency, like a medical crisis, you will have to act alone, and you can do so by law.

 To get a Parental Responsibility Agreement form and instructions about how to complete it go to the Court Service website www.hmcourts-service.gov.uk and in the 'forms' section get form C (PRA1) Parental Responsibility Agreement.

The chart below illustrates how parental responsibility (PR) is allocated

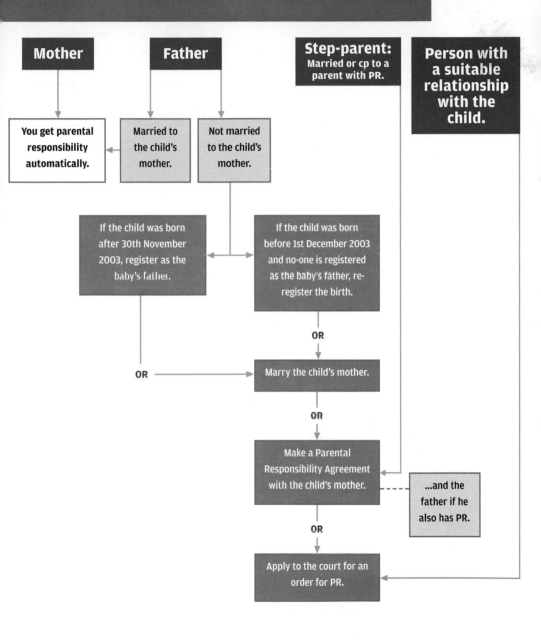

Mother

You get parental responsibility automatically.

Father

Married to the child's mother.

Not married to the child's mother.

If the child was born after 30th November 2003, register as the baby's father.

If the child was born before 1st December 2003 and no-one is registered as the baby's father, re-register the birth.

OR

Marry the child's mother.

OR

Make a Parental Responsibility Agreement with the child's mother.

OR

Apply to the court for an order for PR.

Step-parent: Married or cp to a parent with PR.

Person with a suitable relationship with the child.

...and the father if he also has PR.

The expectation of the Children Act was that, for the most part, parents are capable of deciding matters for their children without the intervention of the courts. Before the Act, in every divorce where there were children orders were made for 'custody', 'care and control' and 'access'. This no longer happens, and the old terms have been abolished (even though they are still used in the popular media). If parents can agree arrangements about where the children will live ('residence') and how they will see the parent with whom they do not live ('contact'), the court will not make any order about this. Orders will be made only where parents dispute the arrangements, and then only if the existence of the order is felt by the judge to be necessary to keep the parents from further dispute (see page 112 onwards for details about disputes over children).

RESIDENCE

You will need to decide where the children are going to make their main home. This is often fairly obvious, with most children staying in the original family home. But other arrangements can be made. If you are going to move them out of their family home, do remember that they will need their own things with them.

Some families feel that the children can have two 'main' homes and divide their time equally

Children's possesions
Children have close and intense relationships with their own possessions. Make sure that they are allowed to take with them whatever they feel they need even if you think that it is unnecessary.

between their parents. If this is your feeling, you need to be absolutely sure that you are not treating the children as an asset that you want to divide equally between you. Children are not commodities. How would you feel if you had to move home every three or four days? Is it likely to be unsettling for them? It is not helpful if you make the decision on the basis of what you feel is 'fair' for you.

Contact

The term 'contact', as used in the Children Act, can mean anything from long overnight visits to telephone calls and letters. There is no single pattern of contact that is laid down or approved in any official way. Each family must make its own arrangements. Whatever you can agree can later be altered to suit changes in, for example, the children's interests or domestic arrangements.

Contact dos and don'ts

- DO keep the arrangements regular, but flexible if need be. It's important that children have a framework and a routine that they can rely on.

- DO plan the contact times ahead together. Keep a large write-on calendar for the children to put stickers on the contact days and this helps them to keep track of their weeks.

- DO remember that in the early days following a split, any contact is better than none. It may not be possible to sort out a regular pattern of contact after you first separate; both your lives may be in too much upheaval. It may be tempting to say that you will not have contact for a while because you fear that it might disrupt the children too much.

- DO keep time. If you agree to collect or return children at particular times, you should stick to them. Similarly, if the children are being collected from you, you should have them ready at the correct time. If something unexpected causes a delay, call and inform the other parent or the children.

- DO NOT use your children against the other parent. Children will know if they are being used as spies, and it is unfair to pull their loyalties in two ways.

- DO NOT behave as though the child's time is a possession you are entitled to. According to the law, contact is the child's right to see the parent, and not the other way about.

- DO use telephone calls as a way of keeping in touch. If you are the one phoning the child, try to agree with your spouse about when would be a useful time.

- DO NOT turn every contact visit into a wild outing somewhere. Low-key activities may be just as pleasurable and valuable for your children. What they want is your time and attention; spending money on them does not compensate for a lack of time or love.

- DO NOT assume that if the children come back from a contact visit cross, fractious or hyped-up, the visit is causing them harm. Children are often like this at the end of any hectic day so don't blame your spouse or the visit. The children may be a little more upset because the hand-over from one parent to another reminds them of what they have lost, but this does not mean that contact is something traumatic that should be avoided.

- DO use all means to stay in touch: if you are the non-resident parent, it is easy to feel that you have lost, or are losing, your relationship with your children. Children are capable of sustaining close and intimate relationships with people that they do not see everyday and using the telephone, email, letters, picture postcards, mobile phones instant messaging can help.

> **"** Try to focus on the long term. Remember that you both have the children's interests at heart. **"**

Contact centres

Contact centres offer a safe space in which parents can have contact with their children in a supervised environment. They are sometimes run by CAFCASS (see page 100) and sometimes by local volunteers. Couples can choose to use them, or a court may stipulate that contact takes place there, for example, if a parent has threatened to take a child away from the parent that he or she lives with and there are worries that the threat might be carried out. Sometimes they can be used in less upsetting cases, where contact has lapsed and the absent parent needs to rebuild a relationship with the child. Using such centres is seldom seen as a permanent arrangement. The hope is that a relationship can be rebuilt and that both parents can come to trust each other again and the children can feel comfortable with seeing the parent whom they do not live with. In any case, some centres, owing to a shortage of space, can offer the service only on a short-term basis.

Make use of mediation, if you can, to resolve disputes. If all else fails, you may have to use the court, but the court too will try to resolve issues by mediation.

Extra Activities

As children get older they may have very full social calendars of their own. They may be involved in after school and weekend activities. Somehow, you need to balance all these, and accept that if you have contact visits at the weekend, you will need to take the children to their activities.

 Parents Apart is a useful leaflet for any parent coping with a separation. Download it from www.advicenow.org.uk

When you can't agree

In any case involving disputes over children, it is wise to consult a solicitor and obtain legal advice. Court disputes are costly, both financially and in emotional terms. There is rarely any winner in battles over who will have primary care of the children on a day-to-day basis.

Wherever possible, you should try to negotiate with your spouse/partner, either directly or through a mediator or solicitors, to avoid a full-blown battle over the children. In such battles, you are forced to lay bare your private family life and will probably find yourself accusing your spouse/partner of not being fit to be awarded the day-to-day upbringing of the child or even to have contact. A bitterly fought court case can make it harder to establish a decent parenting relationship later.

ORDERS THE COURT CAN MAKE

All the following orders are made under section 8 of the Children Act 1989, so they are called 'section 8 orders'. They all restrict in some way the exercising of parental responsibility (see Chapter 4).

Residence order

This settles the arrangements about with whom a child will live, and where. In most cases it will be with one parent, but a residence order can allow for shared parenting, so the children divide their time between their parents' homes. It can also be applied for by two people together, for example a parent and a step-parent.

Contact order

This requires the person with whom the child lives to allow contact with the applicant (the person looking after the child is responsible for making the order work). It can be by way of visits or staying overnight, telephone calls or letters, or all or any combination of these.

Specific issue order

This decides a specific question connected with parental responsibility: for example, which school the child should go to.

❝In all cases, consider carefully whether, from the child's viewpoint, it is best for you to go ahead with an application to the court. ❞

Prohibited steps order

This has the effect of restraining in some way the actions of a person in relation to the child. No step stated in the order can be taken without the consent of the court. This could be used, for example, to stop one parent from changing a child's surname, or from taking the child out of the country without the other parent's or the court's consent.

Both types of order can be applied for in an emergency without the other party having to be notified of the hearing in advance. (Lawyers sometimes call this 'ex parte'.)

The court may attach conditions in certain circumstances to the new orders. For example, it could state that contact should take place only in the home of the parent who looks after the children, or that another adult should be present during the visit.

WHO CAN APPLY FOR SECTION 8 ORDERS?

Either parent can apply for an order, if necessary, even before you have separated or started other legal proceedings. The court orders can be used flexibly, and indeed other people, such as relatives or even the child him- or herself, may also be able to apply where appropriate. The court can make a section 8 order in any family proceedings, thus widening its own powers. It is not supposed to use section 8 orders without proper consideration: court

orders, as mentioned earlier, should be made only if it is better for the children that they are. If the parents can decide between themselves who should look after the children and when the other parent sees them, it is likely that no formal court order will be made and the situation will continue fluidly, with both parents having parental responsibility and thus both deciding together how the children will be brought up. In the vast majority of families, the end result is precisely that – both parents with parental responsibility and no court order.

THE PROCEDURE

An application for a residence or contact order (or other section 8 order) starts when you apply for one to the court, stating what order you are seeking. The application fee is £175. (If you get income support, working tax credit, disabled person's tax credit or legal aid, you will not have to pay the fee.)

The application form (C1 or C2 if you have already started divorce proceedings) asks for all the details of the child or children and asks you to say what sort of order you want made. There is a small section for you to say why you want the order made. This is deliberate; at this stage the court does not want long, detailed evidence filed. If the case cannot be resolved early on, you will have the opportunity to set out your reasons in greater detail.

This chart explains the procedure in the granting of an order under Section 8 of the Children Act

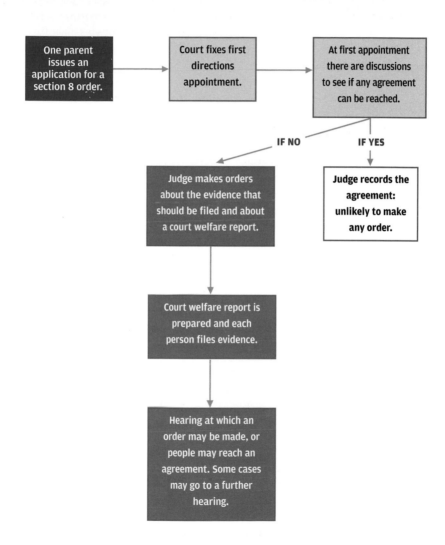

One parent issues an application for a section 8 order.

Court fixes first directions appointment.

At first appointment there are discussions to see if any agreement can be reached.

IF NO

IF YES

Judge makes orders about the evidence that should be filed and about a court welfare report.

Judge records the agreement: unlikely to make any order.

Court welfare report is prepared and each person files evidence.

Hearing at which an order may be made, or people may reach an agreement. Some cases may go to a further hearing.

❝ You may well find during the trial period that you can start to look ahead and agree plans for the future. ❞

The form also asks you whether you have had a Parenting Plan leaflet (see page   ) and whether you have made a parenting plan with your spouse/partner. If you have, you are asked to include a copy with your application.

The proceedings are designed to be accessible to people who are not used to the law. You should fill the form in carefully to ensure that all the facts are correct, But if you ask for the wrong order the court has power to correct an application, or even to make an order that it has not been asked for.

STARTING OFF

The first stage will be that the court will fix a 'directions appointment' or a 'conciliation appointment'. You and your spouse/partner, and your solicitors (if you have them) will be asked to attend an appointment before the district judge. This is in the judge's room, in private, as all hearings under the Children Act are. There will also be a CAFCASS officer, who is someone who is trained and experienced in dealing with children's legal issues.

In most courts you will be asked to go with your spouse to talk to the CAFCASS officer privately. Legal advisers are generally left out of the meeting. The CAFCASS officer will try to explore with you what the issues and difficulties are. He or she will try to see whether an agreement can be reached. This is really a compressed form of mediation, and there will be quite a lot of pressure on you both to try to reach an agreement. For this reason alone, it would be sensible to try to use mediation first, before you get to the stage of filing an application.

Next steps

If you can reach an agreement, then the district judge will be told what you have agreed. You may feel at

Check court fees and get copies of all the forms and information leaflets Children and the Family Courts, Filling in the forms and Serving the form from the Court Service website: www.hmcourts-service.gov.uk

this stage that you want to agree only to a short-term arrangement, to try it out. Most judges will understand, and think this sensible. You could, for instance, agree to a pattern of contact visits for the next three months. The judge can then fix another appointment for the end of that period, and you can use this if you want to.

The judge, together with you and your legal advisers, has to decide whether it would be better to make no order (simply recording what has been agreed in a note on the file) or whether you need an order. The bias is always towards making no order, but if you have had a very difficult time in the past, and one or other of you has not been reliable at keeping agreements, the judge may feel that an order would help you both to know where you stand.

Final decisions

If the conciliation process has not been successful, the judge will decide whether any short-term orders or arrangements should be made pending a final decision of the court. He or she will make an order about who is to file evidence and by when. The judge will also order that a 'children and family reporter' (who is a CAFCASS officer but different to the one seen earlier) should prepare a report about the children. Time limits will be set which must be strictly complied with; the Children Act specifically recognises that delay

Giving clear evidence
In your evidence, try to confine yourself to setting out the facts. 'The facts' can extend to hearsay evidence (information you learned secondhand), but the courts are far more influenced by clear, concise, factual and accurate information than they are by gossip.

may be harmfully prejudicial in a children application. In practice, you may find that, owing to the workload of CAFCASS, the welfare report may take several weeks to be filed. You should also be told the 'return date' – in other words, when the case will next come to court.

The CAFCASS officer will usually interview each of you and the children. The older the children are, the more weight their views will carry. The CAFCASS officer may also make enquiries of the children's schools and other relevant parties – for example, a child's grandmother, if it is proposed that she will be looking after the child while her son or daughter (the child's parent) is at work. The CAFCASS officer will prepare a report which sets out the facts and circumstances and his or her impressions, and occasionally a recommendation to which the court will pay great attention (but will not necessarily follow).

The older the child, the more persuasive will be his or her views. Teenage children in any event often 'vote with their feet' over where they want to live, whereas younger children may find it very difficult to put what they want into words. In practice, the child's wishes are extremely influential. The views of mature, articulate children from around ten upwards, who have

THE COURT'S CRITERIA

The overriding principle of the Children Act is that 'the child's welfare shall be the court's paramount consideration'. In applying this welfare principle, the court has a checklist of matters it must look at in particular. The checklist is neither exhaustive nor exclusive, but one which lays out simply what the court must consider. The court may also consider other factors to be important in an individual case. For example, the parents' wishes and feelings, although not listed, may often have an important bearing on the eventual outcome of a case.

The wishes of the child

The fact that the child's wishes and feelings have been placed at the top of the checklist highlights the child-centred approach of the Children Act: children should, wherever possible, be put first.

❝Children's wishes and feelings will be explored by the CAFCASS officer when preparing the report. ❞

Chlidren Act checklist

- The ascertainable wishes and feelings of the child (in the light of the child's age and understanding).
- The child's physical, emotional and educational needs.
- The likely effect on the child of any change in circumstances.
- The child's age, gender and background, and any characteristics the court considers relevant.
- Any harm the child has suffered or is at risk of suffering.
- The ability of each of the child's parents, and of any other person in relation to whom the court considers the question to be relevant, to meet the child's needs.
- The range of powers available to the court.

> **"Ultimately, and especially for younger children, it is up to adults to make final decisions."**

The effect of change

The courts have long recognised that changing the status quo can compound the difficulties of a child adjusting to the parents' separation. So a parent who is already looking after the children usually has a much stronger claim. This, however, does not apply if the children have been snatched from their usual home environment: the courts can act quickly to return children to the parent best able to care for them. Likewise, splitting the family is almost always regarded as undesirable, so that wherever possible siblings (sometimes even half-brothers and -sisters) should be kept together.

sound reasons for choosing a particular outcome, will often be the decisive factor. But, if the court suspects that children have been coached by one or other parent, 'their' opinions will carry little weight.

Although children's views will be respected, they should not be forced to choose unwillingly between two people, both of whom they love.

The child's needs

If the child is very young, sickly or otherwise needs constant care, a residence order is more likely to be made in favour of the mother. One case decided since the implementation of the Children Act

The judge's role

At a hearing the judge may occasionally ask to see the children in private in chambers without parents or legal advisers present to talk to them and ask them what they want. If so, the court will ask the parents to bring the children along to court (usually this applies only to children of about ten or over).

confirmed the presumption that a baby would stay with his or her mother. It is important to understand that there is nothing in the Children Act that contains a gender bias. It is not unusual, for example, for a court order to provide for older children to live with their fathers. The courts will always look at each individual family: whichever parent has primarily looked after the children and with whom the children have the closer bond is likely to have a residence order made in his or her favour.

The child's age, gender and background

The inclusion of this factor in the Children Act is an attempt to get away from a stereotypical view of

> **" A parent offering a stable home life can be at an advantage when applying for a residence order. "**

the family which does not 'fit' an individual family unit. Each case will be decided on its own merits.

Harm or risk of harm

Alcoholism, drug abuse or violence (towards a partner or children) will prejudice a parent's case. A contact order may be given, but only if it is in the child's best interests (for example, if there were a strong bond between parent and child, if the parent were seeking treatment and if the contact were supervised properly).

Gay and lesbian parents (not to mention bi-sexual and transgendered parents) used to find the courts prejudiced against them. But recent cases show that sexuality is immaterial in the eyes of the court. The most important considerations are whether the parent's relationship with the child is loving, caring and considerate. It is still sensible for a gay or lesbian parent to seek advice from a solicitor experienced in this area. There are several organisations concerned with lesbian and gay parenting.

Risk of abuse

If there is a real and significant risk of harm – such as sexual abuse – the local authority's social services department may become involved and may apply for an order that the children be taken into care. Such a case would become a 'public law' case (where the state, here the local authority, gets involved) instead of a 'private law' case (between individuals) and is likely to be heard in a different court. It is important to appoint a solicitor experienced in public law cases and who is (ideally) on the Law Society's Children Panel (whose members have been trained to deal with such cases).

CAPABILITY OF THE PARENTS

This ranges from practicalities such as whether a parent works outside the home or isable to respond to the child's needs. Overall, it is a matter of assessing which parent can best look after the children during the week (contact orders may be made for the children to see the other parent during the week, at weekends and/or holidays); sometimes the claims of both will be equal. A person's behaviour as a parent will be looked at, but their conduct as a partner will often be ignored (unless it has directly affected the children).

 For solicitors who have experience in gay or lesbian issues try, Stonewall: Tower Building, York Road, London SE1 7NX. 020 7593 1850. www.stonewall.org.uk

Domestic violence

The courts also have powers to make court orders excluding suspected abusers from a child's home – where the local authority wants to take emergency protective action to protect the children. Interim care orders and emergency protection orders are also now available and if domestic violence occurs, children as well as adults can be protected by court orders.

A parent offering a stable home life (especially if remarrying) usually has a stronger claim than an unreliable parent. A parent who abandons the children is likely to be at a disadvantage when applying for a residence order. Where relatives or other people (like childminders or full-time nannies) are involved, their capabilities may also be explored.

A child's right to contact

The chief principle is that it is the right of every child to have contact with both parents and the advantages of regularly doing so are indisputable. A parent looking after children and seeking to deny contact to the other faces an uphill battle.

In rare cases, where the parent looking after the children can show an 'exceptional and cogent reason'

why the other should be denied contact, the courts may accept that, for the time being, contact should not be ordered. The courts have described the process as follows:

The court must ask whether the fundamental emotional need of every child to have an enduring emotional relationship with both parent is outweighed by the depth of harm which the child would be at risk of suffering by virtue of a contact order.

Factors such as actual or potential abuse of a child counteract the in-built presumption towards contact. But where a father has, say, a history of violence or abuse he may be denied contact in any form. In exceptional cases a mother's (or even a stepfather's) hostility to a father having contact has been enough to stop him from doing so, but the court has often insisted that he should have contact via letters or telephone calls. There have also been cases where one parent has been so difficult over contact that the children have been moved to live with the other parent, on the basis that this was more in their interests. However, if a parent is extremely violent or abusive, abuses drugs and/or alcohol, or in other ways will have a harmful effect on the children, the negative effects are likely to outweigh the in-built balance towards contact.

 National Friend: www.friend.dircon.co.uk network of helplines on lesbian and gay issues. Pink Parents: www.pinkparents.org.uk for all Lesbian or Gay family issues.

Other issues that can be brought to the court

The courts can also deal with other issues of childcare between parents and other family members. This section will put the procedures into perspective.

CHANGING A CHILD'S SURNAME

If a child is to be brought up in a new family, a parent (usually the mother) may want to change the child's surname to that of her new partner. Whether there is anything in the law preventing her from doing so depends on the existence of a residence order (or an old custody/care and control order).

If such an order is in force, there will automatically be a provision stating that the child's surname cannot be changed without the consent of the other parent or the court. But if no such order exists, the mother can in theory change the child's surname, as she has parental responsibility which she can exercise independently. However, in practice, where two parents both have parental responsibility, the parent who wants a name change should first try to obtain the other parent's consent. He or she can then apply to the court for permission if the other

parent objects. A parent who objects can in any event apply to the court for a specific issue order. The court application will be decided by the principles that the child's welfare is of paramount consideration and that no court order will be made unless this is better for the child.

The courts have tended to disapprove of changes of name, taking the line that the link between a child and his or her natural parent, as symbolised by the surname,

Changing a child's name

If you wish to change a child's surname by making a deed poll, which is then enrolled at the court, every person with parental responsibility must give his or her consent. However, a name can be changed legally simply by usage, without going to the lengths of using a deed poll.
For further information see the CAB website: www.adviceguide.org.uk

should not be broken, so changes of surname have usually been refused.

However, a mature child him- or herself may apply for a change of surname by way of a specific issue order. If the child has strong feelings about wanting to be included in the new family and sound reasons for making the application, the court may be persuaded to make an order for a change, given that the child's wishes and feelings rank number one on the welfare checklist.

TAKING A CHILD ABROAD FOR A HOLIDAY

If there is a residence order, the usual rule is that a parent who wants to take a child abroad (this includes going from England or Wales to Scotland) should obtain the other parent's written consent first. This is because it is a criminal offence to remove a child from the country without the written consent of both parents or the consent of the court.

Where a parent simply wants to take the child on holiday and has a residence order in his or her favour, he or she can take the child abroad for a period of up to a month. If the other parent objects, an application can be made to the court for its permission by way of a section 8 order. (See also Chapter 7 on child abduction.)

If there is no residence order, the civil law says nothing either to permit or prevent a parent from taking a child abroad. Again, if the parents are in dispute, one or other should apply for a section 8 order. But whether or not a residence order exists, the criminal law still applies.

APPLICATIONS BY GRANDPARENTS AND OTHERS

When a family splits up, sometimes the contact between the children and one set of the grandparents ends, as families divide into opposing camps. This is rarely good for the children: often they can be helped to cope with their distress by grandparents (or other close relatives or friends, say, perhaps a godparent), who can give a helping hand to guide the children through the sad and difficult times.

Grandparents (or for that matter any other interested relative or family friend) can apply to the court for a contact order or other section 8 order. They do not have to wait until divorce or other proceedings have been started.

Before such an application can proceed, you may have to obtain the court's permission. The Children Act gives some categories of people the automatic right to make an application, see box on page 108.

If applicants, such as grandparents, have lost contact with the children over many years and formerly had a bad influence on them, it is possible that their application for permission to apply to the court will fail. The legal test is whether a grandparent can show that he or she has a 'good arguable case' and that there is a serious issue to try. Usually the court will grant permission to apply and leave a full investigation to a proper court hearing involving all sides.

Applications for contact by grandparents are likely to be granted, unless there is deep bitterness between the families which would be exacerbated by making a contact order. Contact orders can be in the form of letters, cards and telephone calls, so the court may make an order for contact in stages, building up contact from letters and telephone calls before a face-to-face meeting, especially if the grandparents have not met their grandchildren for a long time.

Applications for residence orders by grandparents are unlikely to succeed, unless the natural parents (or the local authority if the child is in care) are fully in support and the child has established a pattern of living with a grandparent.

LEGAL REPRESENTATION FOR CHILDREN

Court may not be the best way of sorting out children's problems. It is important to consider mediation or a form of therapeutic help.

Contact rights

You have an automatic right to make an application under the Children Act for contact or another section 8 order if:
- you have had the child living with you for three years or more, or
- you have the consent of the person with a residence order in his or her favour, or
- you have the consent of everyone with parental responsibility (or that of the local authority if the child is in care).

Otherwise, the court's permission must be obtained before the application will be given the go-ahead.

A child can be separately represented in court. This generally happens where parents have opposing views of what a child thinks, and/or their views are firmly opposed.

A child's interests can be represented by a 'children's guardian', a person skilled and experienced in dealing with children, who will put the arguments for what is in the child's best interests. This often happens where the local authority is involved, and sometimes in private cases. The court can also (though rarely) appoint the Official Solicitor to act for the child.

For help and support for grandparents, the Grandparents' Association:
Advice line 0845 4349585. www.grandparents-association.org.uk

APPLICATIONS BY A CHILD

If a child is old enough and sensible enough he or she can apply to the court under the Children Act. Legal Aid can be granted to the child.

Children have brought cases to ask the court for a residence order that they live somewhere else, or for a contact order that the parent who has left the home be made to see them (sometimes against their parent's will). The court needs to be convinced that the child making the application is mature and has sound reasons for asking the court for help, and is not making the application on impulse because of a row with a parent.

APPEALS

Successful appeals against decisions made by the trial judge (the one who originally heard the case) are extremely rare. The judge has a wide discretion, and appeals will be allowed only if the first decision can be shown to be 'plainly wrong'. This is so even if the appeal court feels it would have come to another decision itself. But if further important evidence comes to light, then an appeal might work. If you do go to the Court of Appeal, you may be offered a mediation session to see whether the problem can be resolved out of court.

An appeal against a decision of either the county court (for family cases this is called a Family Hearing Centre) or the Family Proceedings Panel within a magistrates' court will go straight to the High Court. From the High Court an appeal will go to the Court of Appeal.

OUTDATED LEGAL TERMS

Before the implementation of the Children Act, there were three different legal concepts applicable to children: custody, care and control, and access. The legal usage of some of the words was (and is) different from ordinary English usage. Because these terms are still popularly used even though they no longer apply, it is useful to be aware of what they mean. (You may also have an old court order which uses these concepts.)

Custody

This meant the bundle of responsibilities that parents have towards their children, for example, the right and duty to

For children's representation contact Resolution www.resolution.org.uk or the Children's Legal Centre: 01206 872466. Young people call free on 0800 783 2187. www.childrenslegalcentre.com

make major decisions concerning their upbringing, their religion and education.

Sole custody (for one parent).

Joint custody (for both).

Joint custody was the court order that resembled most closely the pre-divorce role towards the children. In a sense, the effect of a joint custody order was primarily psychological, because it confirmed, for the parent who did not look after them, the fact that he or she had a recognised role to play towards his or her children. ('Parental responsibility' now fulfils this function.)

Care and control

This meant the actual physical 'possession' of the child. Orders were made only for the sole care and control: an order for care and control could not be split (unlike the new residence orders).

An order for care and control was granted to the parent with whom the children were living on a regular basis. Even in the unusual cases where children divided their time equally between their parents, only one parent used to have an order for care and control.

Access

This meant the actual visiting periods for the parent who did not have care and control.

Staying access: the child stayed with the non-custodial parent.

Visiting access: the non-custodial parent simply visited or took the child out for the day.

Reasonable access: the parents would agree this between themselves. Where the parents could not agree, the court may have made an order for **Defined access:** determining when the child would visit the non-custodial parent, sometimes specifying even the times when the child should be collected and brought home again.

Child maintenance

If you cannot agree on maintenance, or if you are claiming benefits, you will probably have to use The Child Support Agency (CSA). The law concerning the CSA applies equally to married and unmarried families. In some cases, though, you may not come within the scope of the CSA.

The Child Support Agency

The Child Support Agency (CSA) administers the assessment and collection of maintenance for children under the Child Support Acts. New rules to simplify maintenance calculation came into force in March 2003, with further reforms now proposed to improve performance. This chapter sets out the current system, and also describes what is known of the new proposals and the changes that they will bring.

GETTING ADVICE ABOUT THE CSA

Solicitors and Citizens Advice Bureaux (CABx), as well as and some law centres, should be able to offer advice and help about getting or paying child support through the CSA. Many of them have computer programs which will enable them to check a maintenance assessment or calculation, or work out for you what the likely impact of an application to the CSA would be.

Solicitors can offer a limited amount of advice under the Legal Help scheme (see Chapter 1), but they cannot help you complete the application form or even the enquiry form. They would be able to advise you over particular legal points such as paternity, or jurisdiction.

A solicitor can assist you with an application to court under the Legal Help scheme and could help (but not represent) you in the guise of a 'McKenzie friend' at a CSA tribunal hearing. Legal aid is available for

Parents and non-resident parents

In this chapter the non-resident parent is referred to as 'him' and the parent with care as 'her' – as in the vast majority of cases this is the way things are. However, the Child Support Act makes no distinction over gender, so if you are a male parent with care, the formula and rules will be applied in exactly the same way. Note that 'parent' could be by either blood or adoption. Step-parents are not responsible for the maintenance of their step-children under the CSA, although they may be in divorce proceedings if the children are 'children of the family'.

taking a case about paternity to the courts.

The CSA helpline also offers advice, but you may get only general points answered rather than a particular analysis of your circumstances.

POWERS OF THE CSA

The CSA has the power to calculate maintenance and enforce payment if the following conditions are met:
- There is a qualifying child or children.
- One parent (by blood or adoption) no longer lives in the same household as the child(ren).
- Both parents are habitually resident in the UK.

Challenging the CSA
You cannot have legal aid to help you challenge a CSA assessment through most of the initial appeal stages: reviewing an assessment or appealing to the Child Support Appeals tribunal or the Child Support Commissioner. Only if you get past these stages and have to make an application to the court on a point of law will legal aid be available.

Jargon buster

Terminology and jurisdiction used by the CSA

The non-resident parent (formerly called the 'absent parent') The non-resident parent (NRP) is defined as a parent who no longer lives in the same household as the child for whom the maintenance is applied.

The parent/person with care (PWC) The parent/person with care is the person whom the child lives with and who has the usual day-to-day care of the child.

The qualifying child The child must be under 16, or under 19 but still in full-time, non-advanced education.

Habitual residence The child and both the parents must be habitually resident in the UK. Habitual residence means usual residence with a settled intention to remain. If the non-resident parent is abroad, the CSA cannot deal with maintenance unless he is employed by a UK company, and the court will have to deal with it instead.

McKenzie friend A helper (does not have to be a lawyer) who can accompany a litigator in person in the court room even in a closed hearing but who cannot address the court or examine witnesses.

The Child Support Agency (CSA) website is very clear and informative: www.csa.gov.uk National helpline: 08457 133 133

The CSA calculates the maintenance due to be paid according to the formula laid down in the 1991 Act and in subsequent legislation. It should trace the non-resident parent and pursue him for maintenance.

It has powers to investigate a parent's income and capital. If the non-resident parent does not pay, it has powers to compel payment, the most effective of which is by direct deduction from wages.

The application: who has to use the CSA?

Parents with care who are in receipt of income support and jobseeker's allowance are obliged to ask the CSA to make an assessment of maintenance against the non-resident parent.

If the parent with care is not prepared to cooperate with the CSA, her benefit can be reduced (by 40 per cent of the income-support adult personal allowance, for up to three years).

If maintenance cannot be agreed, the CSA will have to be used as the court has no power to hear a contested application for maintenance and make an order.

 Recipients of working tax credit and of disability working allowance are not obliged to use the CSA

If you would prefer not to use the CSA

Because the CSA has a bad reputation for delay and inaccuracy, most parents with care would prefer not to use it – they would rather keep the threat of an application to the CSA as a fall-back position if negotiations with the non-resident parent are not successful. Parents with care who are not in receipt of benefit can ask the CSA to make an assessment, but are not obliged to. (If there is an existing court order that pre-dates 5 April 1993, the CSA cannot make an assessment unless the court discharges the order.)

It has become a reasonably common practice for couples to agree a basic child maintenance order and have it made in the court by consent so that, if they cannot resolve their differences about

Court order by 'consent'

Though the courts have no power to deal with a new contested application for child maintenance the court can turn an agreement into a court order 'by consent'. The court also still has power to vary a court order. This means that if an order is originally made by consent either parent can later apply to the court for it to be varied either increased or decreased. This application for a variation can be contested.

maintenance, they can later invoke the power of the court to order a variation. Most couples will work out a figure for maintenance along the lines of the CSA formula, but there may be good reasons for deciding on a different amount, depending on the family budget and other parts of the settlement. Thus the effect of the CSA has been to create a two-tier system, with one law for those in receipt of benefit, and a more flexible system for those who are not.

It is partly for this reason that the system is undergoing reform.

Who can apply, when, and how?

You can make an application as soon as you separate from your spouse/partner. You can get an application form by writing to or telephoning your CSA branch office. You can also download it from the CSA website.

Once the application has been made, the non-resident parent will get an equally long form to complete and send back. If he delays for more than 28 days, the CSA can levy an interim assessment, at default rates: £30 per week for one qualifying child, £40 for two, £50 for three or more.

How are payments made?

Both parents will be asked whether their preference is to receive weekly or monthly payments, but the

❝ Either parent can apply for a maintenance assessment, though normally it is the parent with care. ❞

Agency will make the final decision. When the assessment is made, the non-resident parent can either make the payments directly to the parent with care, or to the Agency by direct debit or standing order. The Agency will then ensure that the payments are passed on to the parent with care.

How long does it take?

It is impossible to give a definitive answer to this because it depends on the speed of the specific office of the CSA you use and also how quickly the non-resident parent responds. There has been considerable publicity about the delays in the service and the CSA no longer publish a target time for processing a claim.

When do payments start?

Maintenance liability usually starts as soon as the non-resident parent is notified of the application. However, at this stage liability will not have been worked out and, as it may be some weeks before it is, the liability will build up from that date.

115

> **"** To prevent the build-up of arrears, it is a good idea to start making voluntary payments to the parent with care as soon as possible. **"**

These can either be payments directly to her, or payments for regular household outgoings, like utility bills, or rent or mortgage. You should document these so that the evidence can be produced to the CSA. The amount of the voluntary payments should then be set off against the arrears. You can pay voluntary payments directly to the parent with care, or arrange to make payments through the CSA.

What happens if the non-resident parent does not pay?

If the payments are being made directly to the parent with care, she will need to tell the Agency if they are being made late, or not at all. If the payments are being made to the Agency, it is supposed to chase them if they are more than two days late. It can charge a penalty of up to 25 per cent of the weekly maintenance for each week of late or non-payment and can also take enforcement proceedings to recover payments. The most straightforward way of doing this is

---

Collection service

Under the new rules the CSA offers a collection service to people who have reached their own agreements, but only for collecting maintenance at CSA rates, as CSA assessments would replace the court order or agreement were private payment arrangements to break down. In addition CSA collection and assessment services will be available only after a court order has been in place for at least a year and parents who wish to transfer to a CSA assessment will have to give at least two months' notice. This will allow parents and their lawyers time to renegotiate new voluntary agreements if appropriate.

---

to make deductions from the non-resident parent's wages. Clearly this will not work if the non-resident parent is self-employed. The Agency can also take court action to enforce payments. However, the Agency's track record on enforcement is not good.

CHALLENGING A CSA ASSESSMENT

If you feel that your assessment is wrong, you can seek to challenge it. The first stage in this process is an internal review, which will be carried out by a different Child Support Officer from the one who dealt with your case. If you are still dissatisfied, you can appeal to a Child Support Appeal Tribunal, and thereafter to a Child Support Commissioner; if you feel the decision was still wrong in law, you can appeal further to the Court of Appeal. All this will cost time and probably money – legal aid is not available until an appeal has been made to the Court of Appeal.

❝The court has power to commit a non-resident parent to prison, or remove his driving licence as a sanction, if he refuses to pay.❞

 If you are on a low income you may be able to ask someone from your local Welfare Rights Advice Agency to come with you to the appeal tribunal and help you prepare your case.

APPLYING THE FORMULA

Go to Appendix A on page 239 to see how the CSA formula is applied.

Financial applications for children

If the CSA does not apply to you and your children, you will have to look at other ways of making an application for maintenance for the children. This section will outline some of the options.

As well as reforming the legal framework of the relationships between parents and children, the Children Act 1989 codified the law about financial applications for children. It also enables children over 18 to apply for periodical payments or a lump sum.

APPLICATIONS ON BEHALF OF CHILDREN

The courts retain powers to make orders for stepchildren and other children for whom the CSA cannot act. This includes children whose non-resident parent works – and so habitually resides – abroad (where he is not employed by a UK-based company). Even where the CSA has jurisdiction over maintenance you can still apply to the court

- for an order for school fees
- for the particular needs of a disabled child
- for a 'top-up' order if the non-resident parent's net weekly income is more than £2000
- to vary an existing order
- for a capital sum or a property order.

The orders the court can make for children

- Periodical payments (maintenance). (Periodical payments can be secured, which means that they are guaranteed by a deposit of capital money, but this is very seldom done.)
- A lump sum.
- A settlement of property.
- A transfer of property to the applicant for the benefit of the child or directly to the child (a transfer of property could cover a transfer of a tenancy as well).

If you are in the process of a divorce and your children have been treated as children of the family by your spouse/cp, who is their stepparent, you can apply to the court in those proceedings. If there are no divorce proceedings then you make the application under the scope of the Children Act 1989.

Applications outside divorce proceedings can be made to either a magistrates' court (Family Proceedings Panel), the county court (Family Hearing Centre) or the High Court, although the magistrates' court has power to order only periodical payments or a lump sum.

The court must look at all the circumstances, including the income, earning capacity of the parties (and the financial position of the child), their needs and obligations, any physical or mental disability of the child and the way in which the child was (or expects to be) educated or trained; this approach is often summed up as 'needs and resources'. If you are applying for support from a step-parent then the court must also take into account the level of support the child has had from the step-parent in the past, whether there is anyone else who is liable to support the child, and whether the step-parent has known that the child is not his/hers.

APPLICATIONS BY CHILDREN OVER 18

Children over 18 can apply for periodical payments (like weekly or monthly payments) or a lump sum if he or she is in full-time education or training (although this would also cover situations where the son or daughter was working in the evenings to supplement his or her income while in continuing education). The courts will take the approach as outlined above.

Restrictions on applications

Applications by children over 18 can be made only if the parents (whether married or not) are no longer living together in the same household and there was no previous maintenance order in existence before the child's sixteenth birthday. In other words, this provision is intended primarily for children who plan to go on to further education and whose parents have comparatively recently split up and where the parental part of the grant (for example) is not being paid. Instead of the parent being forced to go to court to chase up maintenance payments, the son or daughter can make his or her own application. Such children can also apply if they are not covered by the CSA, that is, they are 19 or over.

Proposals for reform

The Queen's Speech in November 2006 announced 'My government will take forward legislation to reform the welfare system, and to reduce poverty. A bill will be introduced to improve the system of child support'.

This statement followed the report of Sir David Henshaw on the future of Child Support. The report criticized the present system, and its proposed reforms fall into four main areas:

1. Parents should be able to keep more of the maintenance owed to them. This would mean increasing the 'child maintenance disregard' which is currently £10 per week.

2. Parents should not be compelled to use the CSA if they are on benefit, and should be able to make their own agreements about the level of maintenance.

3. Tougher enforcement powers are needed, which might include the withdrawal of passports.

4. The present Child Support Agency should be dismantled and a new agency/system created. Parents wishing to use the CSA would have to apply to the new agency rather than having the cases transferred.

At the time of going to press, the Government has published a White Paper about the setting up of the Child Maintenance and Enforcement Commission. The earliest date that this is likely to come into operation is given as the end of 2008. Experience suggests that this may well be put back further.

 www.dwp.gov.uk/childmaintenance gives you details of the proposed reforms.

Emergencies

This chapter deals with situations in which you might need the law to protect you or your children in an emergency. It covers domestic violence and abuse and child abduction. The law for married and unmarried couples is virtually the same in these cases. It also covers the steps you can take to prevent assets from being disposed of.

Protecting yourself from domestic abuse

This section will give you clear and practical advice if you have been, or are, a victim of domestic abuse. It covers aspects of the law, as well as places to get advice and sanctuary.

Domestic abuse (which ranges from violence to psychological cruelty) most commonly occurs within the confines of the home, behind closed doors, with no outsider witnessing the event. Domestic abuse cuts across all classes of society. The statistics are dreadful. It is estimated that one in four women will experience some form of abuse. Two women a week are killed by their partners. Men are also (though less frequently) victims of domestic abuse.

Increasingly 'domestic abuse' has replaced the term 'domestic violence', recognising that there is a wide spectrum of frightening behaviour that ranges from outright

Aid agencies

Women's Aid: www.womensaid.org.uk
Refuge: www.refuge.org.uk
Wales Domestic Abuse Helpline:
Phone - 0808 80 10 800
(8am to 2pm and 8pm to 2am)
Rights of Women: Confidential legal advice line for women, run by women.
Phone - 020 7251 6577
www.rightsofwomen.org.uk
Advice for male victims of abuse:
www.mensadviceline.org.uk
Male Helpline - 0845 064 6800
Alcoholics Anonymous:
Phone - 0845 769 7555
www.alcoholics-anonymous.org.uk
Information on substance abuse:
www.recovery.org.uk

 Freephone 24 hour National Domestic Violence Helpline runs in partnership between Women's Aid and Refuge. Phone: 0808 2000 247

violence to psychological abuse. It is possible to be badly harmed without being physically assaulted.

Children may not be directly abused, but will suffer from seeing a parent being abused.

The problem of domestic abuse has received much greater recognition in recent years and there are government initiatives to try to tackle the problem. 'Sanctuary schemes', to give women safe places in their own homes, have been piloted and are likely to be extended. The police, who at one time would refuse to get involved with a 'domestic', now have proper procedures and officers to deal with domestic abuse, and their powers of intervention have been strengthened.

If you are the subject of abuse, you need to take steps quickly to protect yourself, and any children who live with you. Deal with the practical issues of safety first and then take legal steps to protect your rights.

If you are behaving abusively towards your partner, you too need to take fast preventive action, for example by leaving the home or seeking help to stop the abusive behaviour. There are perpetrator programmes to help men who abuse their partners to change their behaviour. Respect is the UK membership association for domestic violence perpetrator programmes.

MAKING SURE THAT YOU ARE SAFE

In principle, and generally, it is tactically better to remain in the family home until either an agreement is reached or court proceedings have been finalised. But in an emergency you may have no choice except to leave home for the time being so as to be safe from injury.

Leaving your home

If possible, take the children with you. If you can't you need to take urgent legal advice about getting back to them. You won't lose your rights as a parent if you have to leave them. However if the children remain with your spouse/partner for a reasonably long period of time, the court might take the view that it would be unduly unsettling for them to move home.

Finding somewhere to stay

If you leave your home because of abuse, there are generally two ways in which you can get emergency shelter, if you cannot stay with

Respect: www.respect.uk.net
Phoneline: 0845 122 8609 for information or you can email Phoneline@respect.uk.net

Essentials to take with you

If you can get away from the home with a bit of planning beforehand, think about taking the essentials that you will need until you can return. Obviously you will need clothes and toiletries, but you might also require the following documents:

- Your National Insurance number.
- Your bank details and savings books.
- Your benefit books or details.
- Your passport and any children's passports.
- Any other personal identification, of the sort that you need to open a bank account.
- Your children's health record books.
- A recent photograph of your partner – in case you need to have court papers served on him/her.

Contact numbers
The contact numbers for refuges are closely guarded, in order to ensure that victims of violence in refuges and their families are not harassed further by their violent partners or ex-partners.

family or friends: you apply to your local authority, or you can look for a place in a refuge.

- Your local authority is under an obligation to provide accommodation for you if you have priority needs (for example, you have young children living with you), and have nowhere else to stay. You will not count as being 'intentionally homeless' (which would allow them to refuse to house you) if you have left as a result of abuse and you are taking steps to return. Contact – by telephone, or in person if you can – the housing department of your local authority or the social services department. The accommodation they are most likely to offer will be a basic bed and breakfast hostel.
- There are a number of women's refuges across England and Wales which provide a temporary home for female victims of domestic violence and their children. Refuge and Women's Aid can advise you about where to go.

MONEY TO LIVE ON

If you can make a planned escape, you should make sure you have some money put away or saved up that you can get hold of once you have left the home. If you have joint bank accounts, think about taking steps to prevent your spouse/partner drawing out all the funds once you have left. You can arrange with the bank or building society that the account is changed so that you both have to agree before money can be withdrawn. As this might be a problem for you in the future, if you want to take money out, make sure that you have withdrawn enough money for your own needs first.

IF YOU HAVE BEEN INJURED

If you have been physically hurt, even if the injury is not serious, go and see your doctor or the casualty department of the local hospital as soon as possible. Make sure that a physical examination is carried out and the injuries are noted on your medical records. Such records can provide useful evidence in court proceedings. Your solicitor may ask the doctor concerned to prepare a report. If you have visible injuries try to get someone to photograph them. Some solicitors keep a digital camera for this purpose. The photographs can be used in evidence.

CONTACTING THE POLICE

Police forces have Community Safety Officers (CSO) whose role is to help and protect victims of domestic abuse. If you call the police for advice, the CSO will probably contact you and explain what can be done to protect you. If you call the police in the middle of, or just after, an incident of abuse they will take steps to protect you and any children as soon as possible. This may involve arresting your partner. The police can also impose conditions on police bail that are designed to keep you safe. If you call the police during a violent incident (dial 999) it is vital that you give your whereabouts, particularly if you are using a mobile phone, as your call

| **Planning point** |

If you have to leave suddenly for your own safety and you have nothing to live on, contact your local benefits office. You may be able to apply for Income Support for the short (or long) term, or get a loan from the Social Fund.

cannot be traced from a mobile. If your partner has been violent or acted in a way that is criminal, then the police can bring a criminal prosecution. The decision about this is made by the police and the Crown Prosecution Service. They act for the state, not for you, so the prosecution is not your choice. They will obviously need your help in any investigation. If you decide that you do not want to make what is called a 'complaint', the matter may stop there. But if there are other witnesses to the crime, a prosecution might be brought without your consent.

GETTING LEGAL ADVICE

See Chapter 3 for how to find a solicitor. Some solicitors in different areas have joined together to run a domestic abuse circle to ensure that a victim can get immediate access to a solicitor who specialises in dealing with these cases. If one firm cannot take on your case, they will pass you on to another. The police or your local Citizens Advice Bureau should be also be able to give you the names of local firms who can help you.

The Family Law Act 1996

Part IV of the Family Law Act 1996 How can it help me?
Get this leaflet from your local County court or download from the Court Service website www.hmscourts-service.gov.uk

❝ If you are a man without children and you have left home because of abuse, your chances of being re-housed are slim. You may have to depend on your own resources or on the kindness of family and friends. ❞

CHANGING THE LOCKS

If you have got to the point where you feel you wish to, or need to, change the locks on the family home, preventing your spouse/cp from entering, or if you have been locked out yourself or are in danger of being locked out, see the chart below for your rights and those of your spouse/cp.

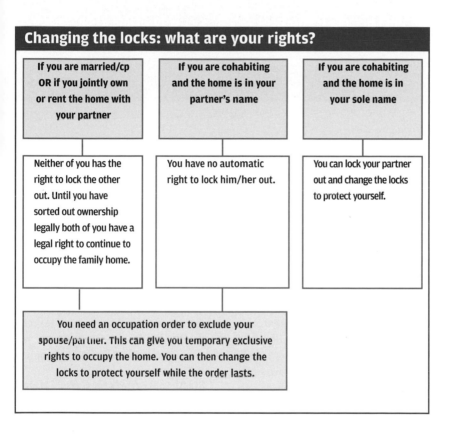

Changing the locks: what are your rights?

If you are married/cp OR if you jointly own or rent the home with your partner	If you are cohabiting and the home is in your partner's name	If you are cohabiting and the home is in your sole name
Neither of you has the right to lock the other out. Until you have sorted out ownership legally both of you have a legal right to continue to occupy the family home.	You have no automatic right to lock him/her out.	You can lock your partner out and change the locks to protect yourself.

You need an occupation order to exclude your spouse/partner. This can give you temporary exclusive rights to occupy the home. You can then change the locks to protect yourself while the order lasts.

See *Which? Essential Guide Renting and Letting* for more details on tenancy law and rights.

Legal steps to protect yourself from abuse

Practical steps to avoid domestic abuse generally need some legal back up. This can range from a stern solicitor's letter to an injunction, backed up, if necessary, by a power of arrest.

You can get legal advice about domestic abuse matters under the Legal Help scheme (see Chapter 1), if you are financially eligible. Legal aid is available (subject to financial eligibility) for applications for an injunction and, in extreme cases, emergency certificates can be issued on the same day.

In 1996 the Legal Aid Board (now the Legal Services Commission, LSC) issued guidance that emergency legal aid would be granted only if the applicant 'is in imminent danger of significant harm'. If you are not eligible for public funding, the cost of getting an injunction is likely to be hundreds of pounds.

❝ If you go to a solicitors' firm which has a legal aid contract, it can decide there and then whether an emergency certificate should be granted. ❞

A solicitor will know about the local networks of support and housing including refuges. He or she can also take various legal steps to help you. You may only need a letter to your spouse/partner pointing out your legal rights and threatening to take proceedings if the behaviour is repeated. It may be more effective to involve the police and have criminal proceedings taken against your spouse/partner. Sometimes this is not enough: you will need a court order (an 'injunction') to ensure that you can occupy your home without being hurt.

LEGAL AID AND INJUNCTIONS

If you intend to apply for legal aid to get an injunction, the Legal Services Commission will want to know whether you have contacted the police and considered writing a warning letter to your partner. If this is going to be more effective than getting an injunction, you will not be granted legal aid. But if this is not appropriate for you, your solicitor can explain this on the application form.

128

The two main court orders: 'injunctions'

A non-molestation order	Orders your spouse/partner not to assault, molest or otherwise interfere with you (or your children). 'Molestation' includes repeated telephone calls, as well as other forms of harassment.
An occupation order	Can order an abusing spouse/partner to leave the home and/or not come within a specified area around it (for example, 100 yards around the home). An occupation order can also allow a spouse/partner back into the home if s/he has left it out of fear of violence and can order the abusing spouse/partner to let her/him back in (and possibly require him/her to leave too). Occasionally, the court may make an order confining a person to a defined part of the home, but this is rarely practicable.

You will need to get legal aid if you need to sort out the occupation of the home.

If you can't afford to instruct a solicitor you can act for yourself and apply to the court for an injunction. You can get the forms and information from your local county court office.

DOMESTIC ABUSE AND INJUNCTIONS

The Family Law Act, 1996, Part IV, covers all applications in all courts for domestic abuse injunctions. Under this law married and cp couples, cohabitants and ex-cohabitants, other family members and people who have lived in the same household can seek the courts' protection.

Which court?

All levels of court can make the orders: it will be up to you and your solicitor to decide which to use. If you have already started off divorce proceedings, it is likely to be the court which is dealing with your divorce case that you will apply to – otherwise it will be the local county court or possibly the family proceedings court (magistrates). Most injunctions are at present dealt with the in county court.

Obtaining an injunction to protect the children

In the rarer cases where it is only the children, rather than an adult, who are at risk, the courts can make an order stopping contact between the violent (or abusive) adult and the children. Social services departments can also take action under an emergency protection order or an interim care order, and can seek an occupation order to oust an abuser (say a stepparent) from the family home.

129

Applying for an injunction

There are various documents that must be filed at court to start off the application for an injunction. This section will help you through the process and procedures.

The documents you will need to complete are:

- An application form, in duplicate.
- A sworn statement in support. In this you have to describe your partner's (and your) behaviour and explain why you need an injunction. You also have to tell the court about:
  o your and your partner's housing needs (and the needs of any children you have)
  o how much money you both have
  o how any order will affect your and your partner's (and any children's) health, safety and well-being; and

If you are not married/cp you also have to include:

- how long you have been living together
- whether you have children or stepchildren
- how long you have been separated
- whether you are in any other legal proceedings together, such as other court proceedings about your family.

Service of court documents

Your solicitor (or you if you are acting for yourself) has to make sure that the respondent gets the court papers. This is normally done by arranging to hand them to him/her personally. This is so the court can be satisfied they have been properly delivered. Often a solicitor will get a 'process server' or a court bailiff to do this. It is helpful if you can give your solicitor a photograph of the respondent and as much information as possible about where he/she works and spends leisure time.

FEES

The county court fee is £60. You do not have to pay a fee if you are legally aided or financially exempt because you are on a low income. You have to complete a further form to apply for the exemption.

Once the papers are filed the court will fix a time and date for the hearing and then the respondent has to be served with the papers. The respondent is entitled to two clear working days notice of the hearing.

Once the respondent is served he/she should produce a sworn statement replying to the allegations. He/she can suggest solutions, such as alternative accommodation, or explain the possibility of remaining in the same house.

Normally the respondent has to be told that you are applying to court. This is a 'with notice' application. An application 'with notice' for an injunction is usually heard very quickly – normally within a few days. However, if the circumstances justify it, you can get an application heard almost immediately, 'without notice', as long as there is sufficient time to sort out legal aid and prepare a sworn statement. Bear in mind that it is very rare that a court will make an occupation order at a 'without notice' hearing.

Before making an occupation order, the judge or court will want to be satisfied both that the circumstances justify such an order and that there is no satisfactory alternative in the light of your spouse/partner's conduct, the children's needs and the available accommodation. Usually the courts require evidence of fairly severe physical violence or intolerable abuse before an occupation order is granted. An occupation order is seen as a draconian remedy. You cannot use it as an indirect way of getting the ownership of the house.

When making an order, the judge has to weigh up the balance of harm as between the victim (and children if they are affected too) and the abusing spouse/partner before deciding whether or not to make an occupation order. In some cases this will mean that the court will want to see whether the abusing spouse/partner will have accommodation to go to if they are ousted from the family home.

Injunctions can be limited to a specific period, for example, three months, or in more severe cases, they may have no time limit. If you are reconciled and resume cohabitation, the injunction can lapse.

POWER OF ARREST

Where the court makes an occupation order or a non-molestation order and where the respondent (the violent partner) has 'used or threatened violence against the applicant or a relevant child', then the court can attach a power of arrest to the order (unless it is satisfied that the victim will be adequately protected without such a power of arrest).

If a power of arrest is given, the applicant or her/his solicitor must make sure that a copy of the order goes to the local police station straight after the court hearing, to notify the local police. At the time when the power of arrest lapses, the police must also be notified.

131

What happens next?

A power of arrest normally lasts for a fixed period of three months. It can last for the same length of time or a shorter period than the order itself. In practice it is the most effective preventive action that can be taken to curb future violent attacks. If, after violence has been threatened, the respondent offers to give an undertaking at court not to be violent in the future, the court is likely to have to consider whether it is satisfied that the applicant (and/or relevant children) will be adequately protected. A court cannot simply accept an undertaking without weighing up its sincerity and the ability of the person giving it to keep his word. In any event, as a power of arrest cannot be attached to the undertaking, a victim should think carefully before accepting an undertaking rather than asking the court for a formal court injunction.

IF YOU HAVE BEEN SERVED WITH AN INJUNCTION

If you know that you are at risk of being violent towards your spouse/partner, whether because you have been violent in the past or because you feel the tension in the house is becoming unbearable, you need to take steps to minimise the risk. Take responsible action, such as leaving the house for a cooling-off period.

If you are served with an injunction or injunction application, read it carefully, together with any other documents given to you, for example the sworn statement. See a solicitor as soon as possible and make an appointment with him or her as much in advance of the hearing date as you can. If you are financially eligible, you can get advice under the Legal Help scheme.

The solicitor will take a statement from you and make this into a sworn statement to be lodged at the court. As an alternative to having an order made against you, you can offer the court an undertaking not to molest your partner. Breaking the terms of an undertaking can invoke just as serious a penalty as breaking the terms of a court order.

Unless you have real grounds to contest your spouse/partner's claim for a non-molestation order, you are unlikely to be able to obtain public funding to be represented in court, even if you would otherwise qualify on financial grounds.

Child abduction

Child abduction is one of the most fraught areas of separation and divorce. Reunite (the National Council for Abducted Children) reports that in 2001, 275 cases were reported to their advice line. Statistically this means that abduction happens only rarely, but when it does it tears the family apart as one parent faces the prospect of never seeing his or her child again.

The Child Abduction Act 1984 makes kidnapping a child a crime. Under that Act, a parent who takes a child out of the country without the prior written consent of the other, or permission of the court, may be committing a criminal offence. There are also civil laws which prevent children from being abducted.

SINCE THE CHILDREN ACT CAME INTO FORCE IN OCTOBER 1991

In the majority of divorces involving children, if a residence order is made, it prevents the other parent from removing the child without consent, but the parent in whose favour it was made is allowed to take the child abroad for periods of up to one month at a time.

WORRIES ABOUT ABDUCTION

If you have fears that your child may be abducted by the other parent (if, for example, the other parent is a foreign national and there are grounds for believing that he or she plans to return to his or her home country with the child), you could ask the court to make a 'prohibited steps' order to state that the other parent cannot take the child abroad without your prior consent or the court's permission. Alternatively, it might be in the child's best interests for a residence order to be made, either during divorce proceedings or later on: this will automatically include an order that the child may not be removed abroad without the consent of the

Reunite (network for parents of abducted children) : 0116 2556 234 www.reunite.org
Department for Constitutional Affairs Child Abduction Unit: 020 7911 7045/7047
www.officialsolicitor.gov.uk/icacu/icacu.htm

other parent or the court. Talk to your solicitor about the best course of action.

IF YOUR CHILD HAS BEEN OR COULD BE ABDUCTED

If you believe that your child is about to be abducted by the other parent, you need to take action quickly. The need for immediate action cannot be overemphasised: as Reunite points out, 'The longer a dispute goes on, the more difficult it becomes to repatriate a child.'

Contact your solicitor immediately. He or she can act to obtain an emergency court order preventing the child from being taken abroad, either via a residence order and/or a prohibited steps order, or by using the old remedy of making a child a ward of court (whereby the court becomes, in law, the parent of the child and no step affecting the child can be taken without the court's consent). The courts can make such orders even outside court hours: a duty judge should always be available. The order should be served on the potential abductor if his or her whereabouts are known.

Emergency legal aid and Legal Help are available, subject to financial eligibility (see Chapter 1).

FURTHER STEPS

In addition to taking legal action, either you or your solicitor should contact the police and ask for a port alert to be carried out. Under this, if there is a real and imminent danger of the child being abducted ('real and imminent' means within the next 24 hours), the police are obliged to notify all airports and seaports of the danger of the child being taken out of the country.

In practice, it is often difficult for officials to recognise and intercept children at ports where there is heavy traffic, and the effectiveness of this action has been lessened since the reduction or near-disappearance of border controls between European Union countries since 1993. To maximise the usefulness of a port alert, provide as many details as you can of the potential abductor and the child, such as full names, addresses, dates of birth, personal descriptions, photographs and (best of all) details of the flight or sailing if you have them.

If your child has been abducted and taken abroad, your remedies are fewer and harder to enforce, but you should still not give up hope. If the child has been taken to a country which is a signatory to the Hague Convention, you should be able to get the appropriate authority to act to have the child returned to you. Even if the child has been taken elsewhere, it may be possible to ask the court in England and Wales to sequester (that is, take away) the abducting parent's property if he or she has broken the court order. This can act as a lever to force the abducting parent to return the child. Ask your solicitor for more information.

Preventing assets being disposed of

Sometimes one spouse/partner will try to hide or dispose of assets before the court can make orders about them. In this way, he or she hopes to be able to frustrate the claims of the other.

Unsurprisingly the courts take a dim view of such dealings and the law gives them powers to prevent such disposals, if they can be caught in advance, or undo transactions to get assets back.

If you think that your spouse/partner will take steps to dispose of assets in this way, you need to be cautious and prepared to take action speedily.

Assess the way your spouse/partner is likely to react to a family split. Has he/she threatened to hide or dispose of assets in the past? Does he/she have shady financial dealings that they would not want investigated? Are there offshore accounts? Do you feel that he/she is likely to be greedy and unscrupulous when it comes to money?

If you have real fears about this, consider what you might need to do before, or immediately after you discuss a family split, to protect yourself financially. It is easier to stop money going, than to get it back later.

 Surrendering a tenancy
If you rent your home and your spouse/partner is a joint tenant with you or the sole tenant, he or she can surrender the tenancy to the landlord and you will not be able to get it transferred to you by a court order. If you want the opportunity to stay in the home you should get a formal undertaking from your spouse/partner that he or she will not make such a surrender. If this is refused, or if you fear that he/she will surrender it to spite you, you can seek an injunction to prevent this, which you can then serve on the landlord.

Practical steps

If you have joint accounts, think about whether you need to make sure that they need joint authorisation before money can be drawn out. If you have a joint credit card, one of you will be responsible for the debt. If it is you, you may need to take steps to prevent your spouse/partner running up debts on his/her card. If you are married and the home is not in your name, you need to make sure that your rights are registered. If you are cohabiting, and the home is not in your name, but you have a claim on it, that claim can also be registered at the Land Registry (once it is issued at the court). You will need to talk to your solicitor and arrange for this to be done.

Legal steps

Along with these practical steps, you may need to take legal ones to obtain an injunction to prevent your spouse/partner disposing of assets. If you think that you may need an injunction you need good legal advice as soon as possible. We would not advise you to act for yourself if this is what you need to do.

You need to bear these points in mind:

- An injunction will be expensive. It isn't worth doing unless the value of the assets justifies it.
- You will have to satisfy the court that there is a real danger of the disposal – a vague fear on your part will not be enough.
- You must tell the court all the facts, including those that might suggest that an order does not need to be made.

If an injunction does seem the best way to proceed, you can make an immediate application to the court 'without notice', without warning your spouse/partner that this is what you are going to do. This is more likely to be effective than an application 'on notice', but it does depend on how unscrupulous you think your spouse/partner is likely to be.

There are two different procedures. If you are married/cp and your claims are going to be within matrimonial proceedings, then you apply under s.37 of the Matrimonial Causes Act 1973. If you are cohabiting then you use the general powers of the civil courts in any civil proceedings. The courts have the powers to freeze assets and also, if the circumstances warrant it (rare in family proceedings), to order a search of home or business premises.

If there has not been time before applying for the injunction to get your financial claims filed in the court, you and your legal advisers will have to undertake to the court to file these as soon as possible.

Getting a divorce/dissolution

The Civil Partnership Act 2004 introduced virtually identical procedures for the ending of a civil partnership to those for ending a marriage. This section of the book applies to married and civil partner couples.

PART 2

The law

The CPA 2004 does not always use the same words for parts of the legal procedure, even when they are the same. A civil partnership divorce is a 'dissolution' in the Civil Partnership Act. However, people may continue to use the old terms (such as decree absolute) and apply them to CPs where appropriate and that is what we do in this book. Thus the word 'divorce' applies equally to the ending of a marriage and a cp.

LEGAL SEPARATION

You do not need to have any formal court order or agreement to be 'legally separated'. If you and your spouse/cp have separated, the simple fact of your separation allows you to describe yourself as separated in any document that you have to complete.

If you think that your separation is going to last for some time before you file divorce proceedings, or indefinitely because neither of you wishes to divorce, then it may be sensible to draw up a separation agreement between you which covers matters such as arrangements for the children, maintenance and property. Mediators and solicitors can help with this. It would be sensible to take some legal advice about the implications of any agreement that you come to (see page 55).

A separation which is likely to be permanent, where neither of you wishes to be divorced, can be formalised by a 'judicial separation' however, this is very rarely used these days.

JUDICIAL SEPARATION

Judicial separation proceedings (CPs can have a 'separation order' which is identical except for the terminology) can be used where a spouse/cp does not accept that the marriage has irretrievably broken down, or does not want to divorce, for religious reasons, for example. The facts that have to be proved are the same as for divorce. The procedure for obtaining a judicial separation is similar to divorce, but there is only one decree, with no interim ('decree nisi') stage.

The effect of a decree of judicial

 The glossary on page 249 explains the jargon and indicates where there are different terms under the CPA.

separation is that the couple are technically relieved of the obligation to reside with each other. But they remain married in law, so that neither can marry/cp anyone else, and on the death of one spouse/cp, the other would be his or her widow or widower. This can be particularly important in the case of an elderly couple, where a wife would lose substantial widow's pension benefits if the couple divorced. The decree does, however, affect inheritance rights: if either spouse/cp dies without making a will, they are treated as if they were divorced.

A decree of judicial separation does not preclude a divorce later, and the facts relied on to obtain the judicial separation decree (except for desertion, which formally ends on a decree of judicial separation) may be used in divorce proceedings. Applications for judicial separation are made much less frequently than applications for divorce. If, ultimately, what you want is a divorce, applying for judicial separation in the meantime can double your costs.

STARTING DIVORCE PROCEEDINGS

You cannot present a petition for divorce until a year after the marriage took place, whatever the circumstances. But you do not have to start off divorce proceedings to apply to the court about problems over the children (for details see Chapter 6). Applications for a residence or contact order, for example, can be made at any time. Similarly, you don't have to start a divorce to ask the Child Support Agency (CSA) for maintenance for the children (or the court for maintenance for yourself). So there is no need to begin an application for a divorce until you have finally made up your mind that this is what you want.

There is only one ground for obtaining a divorce in England or Wales: that the marriage has irretrievably broken down. You have to show that this has happened by proving one or more 'fact'.

There are five facts in all. One of the very few distinctions in law between a marriage and a cp is that CPs cannot use the first 'fact' – adultery - though you can cite sexual infidelity as part of unreasonable behaviour.

Even if you can establish the facts

The facts on which you can base a petition for divorce

1. Adultery and intolerability.
2. Unreasonable behaviour.
3. Desertion for a period of two years.
4. Separation for a period of two years with consent of the other person.
5. Separation for a period of five years.

for going for a divorce now, you might want to consider whether to make a separation agreement with your spouse/cp now and then apply for a divorce on the 'no fault' ground (Fact 4) later. Applying for a divorce when you have lived separately from your spouse/cp for at least two years and where you both consent to the divorce going ahead can help to remove some of the bitterness and difficulties often associated with divorce.

JURISDICTION

Where you were married is not relevant in determining whether you can get a divorce in England and Wales – that is, whether an English court has jurisdiction to hear your petition. What matters is where you live now. The jurisdiction of the court has been brought into line with other European Union countries. One or both of you needs to be habitually resident or domiciled in England or

Scotland and Northern Ireland

The law in Scotland and the procedure in Northern Ireland are different and are dealt with in Chapter 11. Domicile or residence in Scotland, Northern Ireland, the Channel Islands or the Isle of Man is not sufficient to enable you to get divorced in an English or Welsh court.

Wales. You will see this referred to in the court documents as 'England and Wales', which is the legal jurisdictional area.

Domicile indicates the country of your nationality or the country where you have settled and chosen to live. Short absences (for example holidays) can be ignored. You should consult a solicitor straightaway in connection with any proposed divorce where there is doubt about domicile or habitual residence.

Divorce proceedings

Divorce proceedings are usually started in a county court. Not all county courts deal with divorce proceedings, so telephone first to check. This section will guide you through the process step-by-step.

WHERE TO APPLY FOR YOUR DIVORCE

Although you do not have to start proceedings in a court local to you – choosing a court in another part of England and Wales could be useful in sensitive cases or if you want to avoid publicity – it makes sense to go to one that is most convenient for you (and your spouse).

Your case may be transferred to the High Court if the divorce proceedings become defended or, in a very small number of cases, where the financial proceedings or the proceedings relating to the children are extremely complex. In London, the Divorce Registry acts as both a county court and High Court.

EMBARKING ON A DIVORCE

The person who applies for a divorce is called the petitioner. The other is called the respondent. If the basis of the divorce is adultery and the third person is named, he or she is the co-respondent.

In most cases it is fairly obvious who is going to be the petitioner, because generally one party feels more strongly about ending the marriage, and is in a position to say that the other party has been 'at fault', by committing adultery, behaving in an unreasonable manner, or deserting. But it does not have to be as clear-cut as that. Both of you may agree that the marriage is at an end and then you have to decide how best to get a divorce.

Only two of the facts allow you to file a petition immediately: adultery (Fact 1, not available if you are CP's) and unreasonable behaviour (Fact 2). The other three all require a period of separation/desertion of at least two years. If both of you have agreed that the marriage should be ended by a divorce now, rather than after a wait, one of you will have to be the petitioner and the petition (the document that you file at the court) will have to say that the other is 'at fault'. (This does not mean that the respondent will be viewed in a negative light by the court.) The law does not allow you as a couple to present a petition together.

The petitioner is the one who, to a large extent, has control of the timing of the divorce proceedings. The respondent has less to do. This is reflected in the costs: the petitioner's costs are higher than those of the respondent. A petitioner can ask that the respondent be ordered to pay costs, to redress this imbalance.

UNDEFENDED DIVORCE

The vast majority of divorces in this country are undefended and are dealt with by what is called the 'special procedure'. (The term, which is now inappropriate, derives from the fact that the procedure was once applied to very few divorces. It was gradually extended so that all but a very few cases follow this path.) This means that they are dealt with on paper – there are no hearings that you have to attend, unless issues about the children or costs arise. The district judge at the county court will read all the papers that are filed in the case and, provided that he or she is satisfied that the case for a divorce has been made out, the divorce will proceed. Everything takes place in private until the pronouncement of

“There is no public access to the divorce papers. ”

decree nisi, which is made, very briefly, in open court. Again, neither party has to attend.

The proceedings go through a number of stages. The chart on page 154 shows what these are. To make it easier to read, it refers simply to the petitioner and the respondent. In reality, if solicitors are acting for you they will do all the tasks that are shown as things that the petitioner and respondent have to do.

If you decide to act for yourself in the divorce, you can get all the forms that you need for the proceedings by going to your local divorce county court and asking at the counter for them. The court will also give you the helpful information leaflets produced by the Court Service. Alternatively, you could download these, and any forms you need, from the Court Service website.

Fees

Filing a petition for divorce costs £300. The petitioner will also have to swear an affidavit, the fee for which will be between £5 and £9, and pay a further fee of £40 to get the decree absolute. If you receive Legal Help, you are exempt from the fees, apart from the affidavit fee.

If you are acting for yourself and are on a low income or receiving income support or jobseeker's allowance, you can ask the court to grant you an exemption from fees by completing Form EX160. You will still have to pay for your affidavit.

There are fees for other applications, such as those concerning property or children. These are dealt with in the relevant sections of this book.

To start the divorce you or your solicitor need to send, or take, the following documents to the court where you want the proceedings to be. You should always keep, in a safe place, a copy of each document that you have filed.

- Petition:
  - o The completed form of the petition for the divorce.
  - o A copy for service on the respondent.
  - o A copy for service on the co-respondent – if there is one.
- Statement of arrangements for the children:
  - o The completed form of the statement of arrangements for the children, signed by you, and, if possible, the respondent.
  - o a copy for service on the respondent.
- Fee – unless you are exempt
  - o a cheque for £300 payable to HMPG (Her Majesty's Paymaster General), OR
  - o Form EX160 claiming exemption from the fee.
- Certificate with regard to reconciliation:
  If you have a solicitor acting for you on a private, not publicly funded, basis, he or she has to file another form stating whether the possibility of reconciliation has

been discussed with you. If you are acting for yourself, this form does not have to be filed.

- Marriage certificate:
  You will need to file your original marriage certificate or an official copy of it.

GETTING AN OFFICIAL COPY OF YOUR MARRIAGE CERTIFICATE

The easiest way to obtain an official copy is to go back to the Register Office for the area in which you were married, or where you were married. You can apply there by post or in person, and the certificate will cost you £7.

Foreign marriage certificate not in English

You must have it translated and the translation notarised (which means that a special declaration is sworn by the translator confirming the accuracy of the translation). You should look in the Yellow Pages for a translator who can perform this service.

THE PETITION DOCUMENTS

There is a helpful leaflet called D8 Notes for Guidance (D508 for CPs) which is available from the court and the Court Service website. This goes through the petition in detail and explains precisely what should go in each part of the petition form.

If you are acting for yourself in the divorce proceedings, get hold of a copy of this form and follow its instructions carefully. It is important to get all the parts of the petition form correct, because if you make a mistake the district judge may refuse to grant the decree nisi until the error is put right, or further information filed at the court. Court officers may be prepared to help you with the form, but they are not allowed to give you legal advice.

At a later stage in the proceedings you will have to swear an affidavit to say that the contents of your petition are true. If you feel that you have any doubts about, or difficulties with, completing the form, you should consult a solicitor.

Children

All 'children of the family', whatever their ages, have to be named in the petition. Children of the family are, in broad terms, those who are:

- children of both of you
- children adopted by both of you
- stepchildren
- other children who have been treated by both at any time during the marriage as part of the family, but these do not include foster children.

'Relevant' children, who need to be dealt with in the 'statement of arrangements' are those under the age of 16, or under the age of 18 and still in full-time education or undergoing training for a trade,

profession or vocation (even if the child is also earning). If your child is over 16 and under 18, but is in full-time employment or is unemployed (that is, no longer in the education system), it is important to say so, because he or she is no longer a 'relevant' child.

Last things

The last page of the petition asks the court for various things:

- A prayer (request) for the marriage to be dissolved (ended).
- An order for costs to be made against the respondent and/or co-respondent. In a petition for adultery, unreasonable behaviour or desertion, it is usual to ask the court to make an order for costs against the respondent, even if you propose to drop the claim if the petition is not defended.
- Under the heading of 'ancillary relief', orders for maintenance (called periodical payments), lump-sum payments, property adjustment and pensions; such applications are made in general terms at this stage, so you do not need to specify any amounts.

DO NOT cross off the claim for financial relief. If you do it may be complicated or even impossible to apply for it later. You would have to make a special application to the court for leave (permission) to apply later for any required order. Such an application may not be granted if it is made after a long time or if, for example, the respondent says that he or she decided not to defend the petition only because of the absence of any request for ancillary relief. So, even if you have agreed with your spouse/cp that no financial claims will be made, you should still include them in the petition so that they can be formally dismissed by the court. (Only if claims have been made can they be dismissed and a full and final settlement order be made.)

To avoid misunderstanding when your spouse/cp receives the petition, explain to him/her that the claims are being included only so they can be dismissed by the court later. If you have no children, you can delete the part relating to their claims.

Costs

Similarly, you can include a prayer for costs even though you may agree or decide not to follow this request through. What you are claiming here is costs only in respect of the divorce itself (not ancillary issues such as finance or claims about the children). These will be comparatively low, as they are worked out on a standard, limited basis, and are unlikely to cover the full costs of your solicitor.

In the case of a divorce based on periods of separation, the petitioner and respondent often agree that costs will be divided between them, so the petitioner would seek an order for only half the costs to be paid by the respondent. It is possible (but not usual) to seek costs against a co-respondent, but it would still be wise to discuss this with a solicitor.

The last page of the petition should be signed by you if you are acting in person or receiving Legal Help, or by your solicitor if one is acting for you. You should also include the full names and addresses of the respondent (and co-respondent) for service of the petition, and your address. Home addresses can be used, but if solicitors are acting for either or both of you, their address(es) should be inserted instead here.

STATEMENT OF ARRANGEMENTS FOR CHILDREN

You, or your solicitor, must complete a statement about the present and proposed arrangements for relevant children (Form D8A). A blank printed form of statement is available from the court office (or can be downloaded from the Court Service website): you should try to agree its contents with the respondent in advance of starting the divorce, and get his or her countersignature if possible.

If the respondent has not signed the statement of arrangements some courts will want the petitioner to confirm that he or she has tried to obtain the respondent's signature.

COMPLETING THE FORM

This form is eight pages long and requires detailed information about the children of the family. Despite its length, however, it is fairly jargon-free. You will need to set out details about the home where the children currently live, their education or training, any childcare arrangements, amounts of support payable for the children and whether a claim has been made to the Child Support Agency (CSA), contact (access), their health and whether there are any other court proceedings about them. If you do not agree with the current arrangements, any proposed changes should be set out. At the end of the form you are asked whether you would agree to attend conciliation (mediation) with your spouse/cp if arrangements are not agreed. You must sign the form.

The aim of making the form so detailed is to get parents to look in depth at the realities of how their children's lifestyles will change as a result of separation and/or divorce. As the courts cannot ask the parents in person about the children (most divorces now proceed on the basis of paperwork alone), they want to have as complete a picture as possible of the arrangements for the children.

SERVICE OF THE PETITION

The court posts to the respondent, at the address given in the petition, one copy of the petition and of the statement of the arrangements for any children.

Uncertain about the future
If your future is uncertain it may be difficult to complete the form fully. If so, just include as much information as you can, indicating where necessary which arrangements are yet to be decided upon.

The court also sends with the petition an acknowledgement of service form, which the respondent has to complete and return to the court within eight days (although this time limit is, in practice, not always adhered to). If adultery is alleged and a co-respondent is named, a copy of the petition is also sent to him or her, again with an acknowledgement of service form to be returned to the court.

The court has to be satisfied that the respondent (and co-respondent) has received the divorce papers or that all reasonable steps have been taken to serve the documents on him or her. The return of the acknowledgement of service form to the court is normally taken as proof of service. If, however, the acknowledgement of service form is not returned, the petitioner can apply to the court with another copy of the documents and arrange for 'personal service'.

If the petitioner has had difficulty in serving the papers, he or she can apply to the court for the petition to be served by the bailiff of the county court for the area in which the respondent lives, or can employ an enquiry agent (a private detective) to act as process server. This can prove very expensive, however.

If the respondent (or co-respondent) fails to return the acknowledgement of service form but has acted in a way which makes it clear that he or she has received the petition, the petitioner can apply to court for service of the petition to be deemed to have been effected.

If service turns out, in practice, not to be possible, the petitioner may be able to get an order dispensing with service.

THE RESPONDENT

It may seem very hard to be the person who is, on paper, being blamed for the marriage ending but, in practice, this will rarely affect the way in which the court treats the respondent. In issues concerning money the court will consider

conduct only in cases where it is so very bad that it would be wrong to disregard it. A typical example would be where the husband attacked his wife so violently that she was unlikely to be able to work again as a result of her injuries. Adultery will generally not influence the court one way or the other.

DOCUMENTS THE RESPONDENT SHOULD COMPLETE

The respondent receives a set of notes telling him or her about the implications of the answers on the acknowledgement of service form. The acknowledgement of service form is used to prove that the respondent has had the petition. If the petition is based on two years' separation, the respondent is also asked to indicate that he or she consents to the divorce. If you have instructed a solicitor he or she will sign the form. If you are admitting adultery, you have to sign as well. If a prayer for costs has been made in the petition, the respondent is asked whether s/he objects to paying the petitioner's costs and, if so, why. The respondent may have agreed with the petitioner that no order for costs will be pursued against him or her, and a comment to this effect on the acknowledgement of service form should remind the petitioner to delete that request in the affidavit following the petition.

Serving the petition
The petitioner cannot personally serve the petition. Any other person over the age of 16 can effect service by delivering papers to the respondent personally and then completing an affidavit of service and sending it to the court.

147

If the respondent does not agree with the proposed arrangements for the children, he or she should first make sure that what he or she is objecting to are actual proposals and not mere intentions, and should try to discuss them with the petitioner. If there is underlying disagreement, the respondent should send counter-proposals to the court by filing his or her own statement of arrangements.

All financial matters and any disputes about the children are dealt with as separate issues, irrespective of whether the divorce itself is defended or undefended. The respondent has to sign the acknowledgement personally where there are children and a statement of arrangements has been filed.

DEFENDING THE DIVORCE: CROSS-PETITIONING

Defending a divorce is difficult, largely because the sole ground for divorce is that the marriage has broken down irretrievably. If one party is so certain that the marriage has broken down that he or she has filed a divorce petition, it is virtually impossible for the other to say that the marriage is still in existence.

Defending a divorce is also costly. The court fee alone for a cross-petition or answer is £200. It is almost impossible to get legal aid for a defended divorce. Moreover, a full divorce hearing is done in public, which may be humiliating.

However, there are some cases in which the respondent feels strongly, and can prove, that the breakdown of the marriage has been largely caused by the other person's actions, via adultery or unreasonable behaviour. In such cases, the respondent can file a cross-petition. This can be coupled with an 'answer', or denial of some or all of the allegations. A cross-petition must be filed within 29 days of the petition being served.

In most cases, even when the respondent feels that the petition is unfair, most solicitors would advise them to allow it to proceed undefended, because to do so would be cheaper and, in the long run, the respondent will not be placed at any disadvantage in the rest of the proceedings. Where an unreasonable behaviour petition has been filed, the acknowledgement of service form asks the respondent: 'Do you intend to defend the proceedings?'. One way of reserving the respondent's position is for him or her to answer: 'No. But I do not admit the truth of the petitioner's allegations of behaviour made against me in the petition.' This is not a defence, but the respondent can then feel that he/she has not admitted that the allegations are true.

Next steps

If a cross-petition is filed, the divorce goes ahead on the basis of the cross-petition (if the petitioner does not dispute it), or cross-decrees (where each party gets a decree on the basis of the 'fact' that he/she has alleged).

If the petitioner disputes the allegations made in the cross-petition, he/she can file a 'reply' at the court. The case cannot proceed under the 'special procedure' – instead, either party can apply to the court for 'directions for trial'. Normally, this means a private hearing at which the district judge sees if any agreement can be reached so that the case can proceed undefended. Only if these efforts fail will the district judge allow the case to go forward to a hearing of the divorce. In practice only a tiny number of defended divorces proceed to a full hearing.

The full divorce hearing will be in open court before a judge. Each party should instruct his/her own solicitor, who may instruct a barrister for representation in court.

GETTING BACK TOGETHER

Some couples find that there is a chance of saving the marriage when the divorce procedure is well under way, but feel that they are bound to continue with the court action until the end. This is not necessary.

It is best to tell the solicitor and the court what is happening if your spouse/cp wants to give the marriage another try too. You can apply to the court to dismiss the petition when you feel the reconciliation is working. It is especially important to tell the court if you have obtained an order to get or keep your spouse out of the house and/or not to molest you. Such an order will automatically lapse once you start living together again.

Studies of divorced couples suggest that some regret the decision to get divorced, and many start to feel uneasy about the process long before getting the decree – but feel unable to halt it once it has begun. Remember that it is you who must make decisions, not your solicitor. If you are unsure about going ahead with a divorce you can call a halt (if you are the petitioner), as long as you do so before decree nisi (although even a decree nisi can be rescinded by an application to the court).

You may want to consider whether some or all of the differences with your spouse can be resolved with outside, non-legal help. A fresh viewpoint can often be useful. Such help can, for example, be obtained from a relationship counsellor (such as Relate); see also Chapter 4.

Stop if you want
The proceedings are not a rollercoaster - you can pause them or stop them altogether. Do this if you feel at any stage that you both might like to give the marriage another try.

Continuing divorce proceedings

Once the respondent has been served, the next stage in getting an undefended divorce is to apply to the court for a date for the decree nisi to be pronounced, by completing the 'request for directions for trial (special procedure)' form.

SPECIAL PROCEDURE

The petitioner can make this application only if he/she can prove that the respondent and any co-respondent have been served with the petition and have had the opportunity to defend it. Usually, the respondent's filing of the acknowledgement of service is taken as proof of service. The court then sends a copy of the acknowledgement to the petitioner, usually together with a blank form of 'request for directions for trial' and a blank form of affidavit. The court also normally sends a helpful leaflet (D186, The respondent has replied to my petition – what must I do now?), which can be downloaded from the Court Service website.

The petitioner must complete the 'request' and swear the affidavit and lodge them with the court. In the 'request' form, the petitioner should fill in only the top part by inserting the name of the court, the number assigned to the petition, the names of the petitioner and respondent, and then dating and signing it. The rest of the form is completed by the district judge and court staff.

AFFIDAVIT IN SUPPORT OF THE PETITION

The 'special procedure' affidavit is a fairly straightforward document, mostly in the form of a questionnaire. The questions refer to the petition, asking for confirmation that its contents are true and for any alterations or additions. (Knowingly giving false information is perjury, which is a criminal offence.) The petitioner also has to state whether he or she is going to pursue any requests for costs made in the prayer of the petition.

There is a slightly different form of affidavit for each of the five facts on which a divorce can be based.

If the respondent has signed the acknowledgement personally, a copy of it must be 'exhibited' to the affidavit (attached and sworn with it). Similarly, if the respondent has signed the statement of arrangements for the children, the signature must be identified. The fee for swearing an affidavit is £5 plus £2 for each document exhibited.

You can swear the affidavit in front of a solicitor (other than the one acting for you), a commissioner for oaths or the court office. Most solicitors' firms are very willing to offer this service and you can go to a firm convenient for you.

The completed affidavit, signed and sworn, has to be sent or taken to the court with the application form requesting directions for trial.

You do not need to serve the respondent, or notify him or her that you are doing this, but normally it would be courteous to do so.

DISTRICT JUDGE GIVING 'DIRECTIONS FOR TRIAL'

Provided that the district judge is satisfied about the service of the petition on everybody concerned, that an opportunity for defending has been given and, in a case based on two years' separation with consent, that the respondent's consent has been confirmed, and that all the paperwork is correct, he or she will give directions for the case to be entered in the special procedure list.

If the district judge is not satisfied with the information in the petition or affidavit, the petitioner (or a witness) may be asked to lodge a

&&If the district judge still does not accept that there is sufficient evidence for a divorce, he or she may direct that the petition be removed from the special procedure list. 99

further affidavit or give additional information on the points of concern.

A fresh application then has to be made for directions and for a date to be fixed for a hearing in open court before a judge.

When the district judge is satisfied that there is sufficient evidence to support the petition, he or she will certify that the petitioner is entitled to a decree nisi of divorce (or decree of judicial separation). The court office will then fix a date for the judge to pronounce the decree nisi.

About the children

At the same time that the district judge looks at the divorce papers, he or she must also consider the arrangements for the children and decide whether no order is better for the children. (The rule is that the court will incline to making no order, unless it is plainly better for the children that an order be made. See Chapter 5.) If the judge so decides, then a certificate of satisfaction will be issued to that effect and the decree nisi pronouncement will go ahead.

If, however, the district judge has doubts or concerns about proposals for the children, or if there is a clear dispute between you, then further evidence will usually be called for. The judge can ask both of you to attend a special appointment at court, or for affidavits or a welfare report to be filed. In that case the decree nisi will usually be postponed until the district judge is again satisfied that no court order needs to be made, or that a residence and/or contact order will be made where appropriate.

DECREE NISI (CONDITIONAL ORDER)

You will both be sent a form with the date of decree nisi. The general practice is that the court will have a list of decrees to be pronounced on a particular day. This takes place very quickly, normally as the first thing after the court starts in the morning, in a court that is open to the public. The court clerk simply reads out a list of the surnames and the judge utters a few brief words to pronounce all the decrees. You do not need to be there.

After the pronouncement the court sends a copy of the decree to each of you.

DECREE ABSOLUTE (DISSOLUTION ORDER)

The decree nisi is a provisional decree and does not end the marriage. It entitles the petitioner to apply to the court for the decree to be made absolute after a period of six weeks and one day have elapsed. Until that is done, you are still legally married.

The respondent must be given notice of the application by the petitioner. An application will be granted only in urgent circumstances, for example to enable one of the couple to marry again before a child is born.

Issues over divorce costs
If there are issues about costs the judge will hear these in the same sitting as the pronouncement of the decrees. These arguments are normally quite short. You or your solicitor will need to be there if you have not sorted out who is to pay the divorce costs by this stage.

Emergency decrees
In an emergency a decree can be made final earlier than the six weeks if the petitioner applies for this when the decree nisi is pronounced and attends to explain to the judge in person the reason for the application.

The procedure

To apply for a decree absolute the petitioner completes the application form (obtainable from the court office) by:

- inserting the date of the decree nisi
- dating the application
- signing the form
- lodging this form, together with a fee of £40 (or another exemption from fees form, EX160) at the court office.

The court checks the file to make sure everything is in order and then issues the certificate of the final decree. It is sent to the petitioner and respondent, normally in a day or two. If there are very urgent reasons for getting the decree absolute immediately, you can ask the court office if it

> **❝ It is important to keep your certificate of decree absolute in a safe place. You would, for example, certainly need to produce it for the registrar or priest if you ever wanted to marry again. ❞**

when the time comes, after a further three months have elapsed (that is, six weeks and one day plus three calendar months after decree nisi), the respondent may apply to the district judge for the decree to be made absolute, with an affidavit setting out the reasons why it is he or she rather than the petitioner who is applying. This will result in a hearing at which the district judge will decide whether the decree should be made.

If decree absolute has not been applied for within 12 months of the decree nisi, the delay must be explained when the application for decree absolute is lodged, giving the reason for the delay and stating whether the couple have cohabited since decree nisi and whether there are any more children. A district judge may require further explanation or even affidavit evidence before the decree is made absolute and final.

Abroad

If you want your decree absolute for use abroad - for a remarriage say - you will need to get the document specially signed by the district judge so that the document can be legalised at the Legislation Office at the Foreign and Commonwealth Office in London.

---

will do this for you, explaining your reasons.

If the petitioner does not apply for the decree nisi to be made absolute

Divorce: the legal steps

Follow these steps to see how the divorce procedure works.

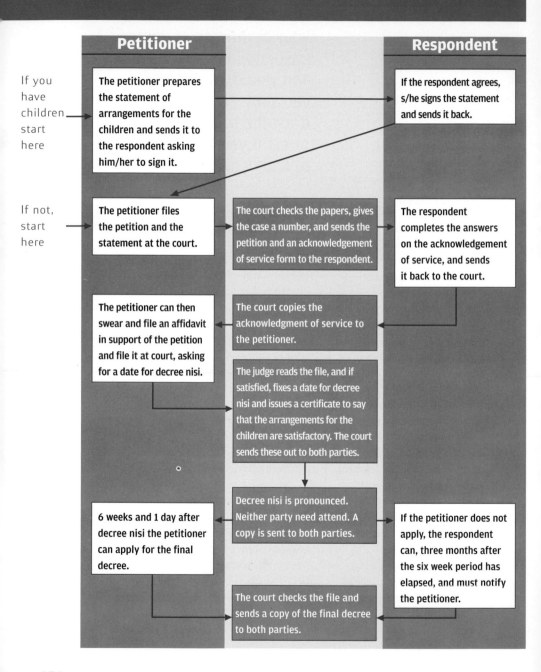

Petitioner

Respondent

If you have children start here

The petitioner prepares the statement of arrangements for the children and sends it to the respondent asking him/her to sign it.

If the respondent agrees, s/he signs the statement and sends it back.

If not, start here

The petitioner files the petition and the statement at the court.

The court checks the papers, gives the case a number, and sends the petition and an acknowledgement of service form to the respondent.

The respondent completes the answers on the acknowledgement of service, and sends it back to the court.

The petitioner can then swear and file an affidavit in support of the petition and file it at court, asking for a date for decree nisi.

The court copies the acknowledgment of service to the petitioner.

The judge reads the file, and if satisfied, fixes a date for decree nisi and issues a certificate to say that the arrangements for the children are satisfactory. The court sends these out to both parties.

Decree nisi is pronounced. Neither party need attend. A copy is sent to both parties.

6 weeks and 1 day after decree nisi the petitioner can apply for the final decree.

If the petitioner does not apply, the respondent can, three months after the six week period has elapsed, and must notify the petitioner.

The court checks the file and sends a copy of the final decree to both parties.

Summary of terms

Acknowledgement of service Form sent by the court to the respondent (and co-respondent, if any) with the petition, with questions about his or her intentions and wishes in response to the petition; its return to the court establishes service of the petition.

Adultery Sexual intercourse by a husband or wife with someone of the opposite sex at any time before a decree absolute. Not applicable to cp.

Affidavit A statement in writing containing a person's evidence, on oath or by affirmation.

Ancillary relief General term for the financial or property adjustment orders that the court can be asked to make 'ancillary' to a petition for divorce or judicial separation.

Answer The defence to a divorce petition, denying the allegations in the petition or cross-petition.

Child of the family Any child of both the parties and any child who has at any time been treated by both the parties as a child of their own (but not foster-children); has to be listed in the petition irrespective of age. 'Family' in this context means married family.

Clean break A once-and-for-all order that deals with all financial issues between spouses, provides for the dismissal of maintenance claims and is not capable of subsequent variations even if circumstances change.

Consent order Order made by a court in terms agreed by both parties.

Contact (formerly termed access) An order under the Children Act for the child to visit or stay with the parent with whom the child is not living, or to exchange letters, cards or telephone calls; contact orders may also be made in favour of non-parents, e.g. grandparents.

Co-respondent The person with whom the respondent has committed adultery. Not applicable to cp.

Cross-decrees When a petitioner is granted a decree on the basis of the petition and the respondent on the basis of the answer.

Cross-petition When the respondent puts forward different reasons for the breakdown of the marriage from the petitioner's, and seeks a divorce on those facts.

Decree absolute (CP: dissolution order) The final order dissolving the marriage.

Decree nisi (CP: conditional order) Document issued once the court is satisfied that the grounds for divorce are established, allowing the petitioner to apply to have the decree made absolute after a further six weeks and one day. It does not end the marriage.

Summary of terms

Directions for trial The stage of divorce proceedings when the district judge considers the petition and affidavit in support, and requests further information if required, before giving his or her certificate for a decree nisi to be pronounced.

Petition The document that asks the court to end the marriage.

Petitioner The person who initiates divorce proceedings by filing the petition.

Prayer Formal request in the petition, or answer, for the court orders which the petitioner or respondent seeks; for example, dissolution of the marriage, orders under the Children Act, costs, ancillary relief.

Respondent The spouse who is not the petitioner or the applicant.

Special procedure In an undefended divorce, the decree can be issued without either petitioner or respondent having to appear (or be represented) at the court. The facts submitted by the petitioner in the petition and verified on affidavit are considered by the district judge. When he or she is satisfied that the facts in the petition are proved and that ground for a divorce exists, he or she issues a certificate to that effect and fixes a date for the formal pronouncement of the decree nisi by the judge. A copy of the decree is sent through the post to both husband and wife by the court office.

Statement of arrangements Form which has to be filed with the petition if there are relevant children of the family, setting out arrangements proposed for them in the future; this should be agreed with the respondent and countersigned, if possible, before the divorce is started.

Undefended divorce Where the dissolution of the marriage and how it is to be achieved are not disputed (even if there is dispute about ancillary matters such as the children or finances)

Money in divorce

This chapter describes how you go about working out a fair division of your assets. It tells you about the recent trends in divorce law and the principles used by the courts when making decisions about financial matters.

Working out who gets what

This section will give you some guidance on what to expect and how to deal with some of the procedures.

People often make two incorrect assumptions about finances in divorce. These are:

- That there must be a legal formula for working out the division of assets and level of maintenance after divorce;
- That in every case, a judge will decide how the assets are to be divided.

Both are wrong. The only formula for working out a financial settlement in family law is the Child Support Agency's (CSA's) formula for the maintenance of the children. (This will not apply to children of cp couples unless they are adoptive parents.) Apart from this formula, each case is decided on its own circumstances. What suits one family may not be best for another, even though, superficially, they seem alike. There are clear criteria laid down by law and an experienced lawyer can give you an idea as to the sort of order that a court could make in your case.

If you reach agreement about finances, it would still need to be made into a court order, but it is made 'by consent', which means that you send the formal terms of the order to the court and the judge approves them, making them into a binding order. Very few cases go all the way to a fight in court, and most that start off like this are settled at some stage in the proceedings.

A court order is the 'bottom line' when you are negotiating – in other words, it's what you will end up with if you cannot reach a settlement.

The courts no longer have a free rein in deciding how the family income can be divided, as the CSA usually has jurisdiction over child support (where there are children covered by its jurisdiction). After that has been worked out, the lawyers (and ultimately the courts, if the case proceeds to a full hearing) will

“In most cases it is the couple together with the help of their mediators and/or lawyers, who work out the settlement of the finances.”

Financial advice
It makes sense to consult a solicitor about money, even if you feel that you can deal with the basic divorce proceedings yourself.

"The judge is not concerned to reward or penalise one party or the other for behaviour during the marriage. The law does not require it. "

examine how much is left for division and will apply the court-based guidelines.

The other important questions are:
- With whom the children should live (in cases involving them),
- Whether the family home needs to be kept.

Many people believe that each asset owned by the couple has to be split down the middle. This is not usually the case. Instead, each person will keep some assets, and you will try to balance them out to achieve a fair division. A wife, for instance, might keep the house, and the husband his pension fund. One of them might take the shares and the other the endowment policy.

The judge will be looking forward, trying to ensure that any children are properly looked after, and that both parties are provided for in the future.

Trends and developments

In the last year or so, a number of divorce cases have attracted a good deal of media attention, largely because they have involved very rich couples.

It is hard to generalise about how finances are sorted out during a divorce because each case turns on its own set of facts, and there are no legal formulas to guide settlements. It is also hard to use cases involving the very rich as guidelines for families with average, or below average resources. However, there has been a discernable shift in attitude in recent years.

In a marriage that has lasted a reasonable length of time, particularly where there are children, the courts are open to looking at an equal division of the capital assets as a starting point. Also, the courts have clearly recognised that a non-earning contribution to the marriage should be given a financial reward. This does not mean that in every case a couple will be expected to divide everything up equally, but in practice that can be your starting point and then you consider reasons why an equal division might not be fair.

Typical reasons might be that a half share will not adequately cover the needs of a parent with whom the children are going to live, or that one of the couple has contributed by far the larger share of the wealth. For most families the first thing to sort out is future living needs and costs. If these can be adequately met by half shares then this might feel fair. However, for most families, there is not enough capital to split in this way, and ensure at the same time that the children have a roof over their heads. This means that you will not be able to achieve an equal division.

Civil partnerships

The Civil Partnership Act 2004 introduced a new field of family law but it is too early to say whether the courts will apply existing case law to civil partnerships. In theory there is no reason why a distinction should be made. The factors that the court has to take into account and the powers of the court to make orders are the same as those for married couples. Any CPs that split up in the next five years, say, are going to be treated as short marriages, however, many may have had a long period of cohabitation beforehand which the court will generally take into account. In general therefore any established principles in the field of matrimonial law could be assumed to apply equally to CPs.

What the court considers

In deciding whether to make financial orders on a divorce, and if so, what orders the law says that courts must take account of a list of criteria.

No one factor outweighs the others but as a general rule, the welfare of any child is an over-riding consideration when weighing up the various factors.

If you are your children's biological or adoptive parents, the court has only limited power to make orders for them (other than consent orders). But it can still make 'top-up' orders, or orders for disabled children, or stepchildren if they have been treated as 'children of the family'. It can also make lump sum orders. Before deciding on the amount of any order for children, the district judge will look

The criteria that the court must consider

Marriages, s.25 Matrimonial Causes Act 1973 (as amended); CPs, Schedule 5 Part 5 Civil Partnership Act 2004

- the financial resources of both spouses/CPs, both now and in the foreseeable future, including any increased earning capacity which the court could reasonably expect either person to try to acquire
- the financial needs, obligations and responsibilities of both spouses/CPs, both now and in the foreseeable future
- the standard of living before the breakdown of the marriage
- the ages of both spouses/CPs
- the length of the marriage
- any physical or mental disabilities
- the contributions of each spouse/cp to the welfare of the family including any contribution in caring for the family or looking after the home, both in the past and in the foreseeable future
- in some circumstances, the conduct of either spouse/cp
- the value of any benefit, such as a pension, which either spouse/cp would lose the chance of acquiring as a result of the divorce.

The criteria for orders for children

- the gross income of each parent and any necessary expenses of his/her work that can properly be set against their gross income, together with any future earning capacity
- the needs of the children, now and in the foreseeable future
- the needs and outgoings of the two adults
- the possibility of each being financially self-sufficient
- the effect of tax on any proposed order
- the effect of any order on welfare benefits entitlements.

> **"If a spouse/cp is felt to be unreasonably refusing to work when there are job opportunities available, their maintenance order might be reduced."**

first at the shortfall between the child support and the needs of the parent looking after the children. Factors particularly relevant to children's maintenance are:

In all cases, the overall question of costs must be considered.

Most factors that the court must consider are straightforward and need no extra explanation. The following need a little more detail:

- Earning capacity: The court is specifically directed to consider whether either spouse could reasonably increase his or her earning capacity. Courts recognise that women who have long been out of the job market due to childcare for example, may not be able to make an immediate return. A woman who has not worked outside the house throughout the marriage, who has grown-up children and is herself only a few years from retirement age, is recognised as having a very limited earning capacity, perhaps none. The

extent to which it might be reasonable to expect her to find paid employment would depend very much on how realistic an option this is, set against the background of the marriage, the husband's earnings, her health, her tangible job prospects and all the other circumstances. Her requirement for a form of pension, to cover her maintenance needs after retirement age, will also need to be taken on board.

- Conduct: The court is directed to consider conduct if it is such that, in the opinion of the court, it would be inequitable to disregard it. Only in exceptional cases will conduct be brought into account, and then only where one person's conduct has been 'gross and obvious' while the other's conduct has been comparatively blameless.
- New relationship: The court will take into account a new relationship formed by either of you. If either or both of you have formed a new relationship and are moving out to live with the new partner, the break-up of the marriage may be less damaging financially and as far as accommodation costs are concerned.
- Length of marriage: The question of whether the court should take into account any time of premarital cohabitation when making an order has

162

caused some legal controversy. It is likely to be taken into account if children were born during that period, or if one party had made a substantial financial contribution to the shared home before marriage. It is likely to be considered under the provision dealing with 'all the circumstances of the case' rather than the factor relating to length of the marriage. In the case of cp couples, where there may have been many years of cohabitation before the partnership could be legally recognised, the court is likely to take into account the extent to which the partnership was committed and finances were combined.

How orders are worked out

This section aims to show how you as a couple can work out an agreement, what your lawyers will be doing when they advise you and what the judge will be doing if it goes all the way to a final hearing.

WORK OUT THE TOTAL FINANCIAL PICTURE

You both need clear and full information about each other's finances. This is the point of the information gathering we set out in Chapter 2. You are obliged to be honest with your ex about your position. Each of you is entitled to 'full and frank' disclosure from the other. If you don't provide this voluntarily, the court has powers to compel you to tell, which you can invoke.

All assets, however you acquired them, are matrimonial assets. That doesn't necessarily mean that they will be split up between you, but they must be taken into account in reaching a final settlement.

Case Study Sam and Ali

Asset	Joint	Sam's	Ali's
House, worth £150,000 less outstanding mortgage £95k	£55,000		
Endowment: current surrender value	£8,500		
Shares		£5,000	£2,000
Savings	£6,000	£555	£10,000 (inherited from parents)
Car	£5,000		
Assets	**£74,500**	**£5,555**	**£12,000**
Less debts			
Credit cards		£1,500	£695
H.P. (car loan)	£4,500		
Net Totals	**£70,000**	**£4,500**	**£11,305**
Pensions: CETV		£15,000	£3,000
Income (gross a year)		£24,000	£15,000

WORKING OUT FUTURE NEEDS

Housing is probably the biggest consideration; once you have settled on what you want to do, most of the other decisions fit round this. It's important to make sure that you work out the cost implications of any plans, both in terms of the capital you will have to spend and the your future income needs. Don't lose sight of what will happen when you and your ex reach retirement age. Pensions are an important factor in divorce settlements. Statistics show, worryingly, that after a divorce women's income decreases on average by 17%, while men's increases by 12%.

MATCHING RESOURCES AND EXPECTATIONS

Once you know what there is to share, and you have an idea of what you want for the future, you can start to think about how the assets might be divided up. You have to bear in mind the criteria

Expectations

Most families will find that this is the difficult part because the assets that sustained one family cannot easily stretch to two. Both of you will probably be poorer, at least in the short term, than you were together.

> **"** Fairness also has to take account of what you as a couple might have expected out of the marriage if you had not split up. **"**

used by the court. You are trying to match needs with resources and then achieve an overall fairness.

FAIRNESS AND COMPENSATION

Fairness does not necessarily mean equality. As we described on page... the courts have moved towards 'the yardstick of equality' in recent years. This does not mean that this is the right division in all cases.

The main factors that will militate against an equal split will be if:

* the lion share of the wealth has been created by one person
* one person brought a large share of the wealth into the marriage, by, say, an inheritance
* one person is financially dependent on the other and will suffer if he/she is not supported in the future. This factor can also prevent a clean break settlement. A typical example of this would be the wife who has, as a joint family decision, given up her career to look after the children and run the

home. She has done this for many years and has as a result made no pension contributions of her own. She has also lost out in the job market and would have to retrain before she could go back to work. She had a reasonable expectation that in her old age she would be supported by her husband and his pension. Any settlement or court has to take this into account and make sure that she is provided for in the future. This means that there is an element of compensation for the lost expectations.

IF YOU HAVE CHILDREN

Their needs come first. They need maintenance and they need a home. If the CSA applies to you, there may not be much room for discussion about the amount of maintenance. But, unless the parent the child lives with is on benefit, you do not have to use the CSA. You might use the formula as a guideline, but you can agree a different amount, higher or lower, depending on what you can afford, and what the children's needs are. See chapter 6 for more information on child maintenance.

PRE-NUPTIAL AGREEMENTS

'Pre-nups' have become increasingly popular in recent years. In many countries they are a normal part of married life and they are legally enforceable, but this is not the case here. The courts will not let couples 'oust' the courts' right to make financial orders in this way. However, they are not entirely worthless. If a couple has been honest with each other about their finances before marriage, and have made fair and sensible promises to each other about what they will expect to have if the marriage breaks up, then you may both feel that you will stick to this and thus avoid the need for a legal argument. This will save you costs and make things easier.

If you have no children

A couple with no children who are financially independent of each other may find it easier to divide their assets.
If the marriage is relatively short a couple might expect to each take what they brought into the marriage, divide any jointly acquired assets evenly and achieve a clean break. The longer the marriage, and the more finances have been intermingled, the greater the tendency to an equal division will be, provided this means that the needs of each are met.

❝ If you do disagree and come to court for a ruling, a judge might find your pre-nuptial agreement persuasive. ❞

If you have children there will almost certainly be maintenance for them but you can still have a clean break between the adults.

AIMING FOR A 'CLEAN BREAK'

The court is, by law, biased in favour of achieving a 'clean break' order if possible. And most couples would generally prefer this sort of arrangement too. A clean break is an order where the couple are not left with any continuing future obligations to each other. **This means that it cannot include maintenance payments.**

When aiming for a clean break, you have to consider whether one of you has a maintenance claim against the other. If she or he has, the order should aim to 'compensate' for the loss of this claim by increasing her or his share of the capital. There are various established ways of working out what the appropriate capital sum should be. You have to bear in mind that there might not be enough capital to do this, however much you might want to.

Although a financial order is in most cases a 'one off', so you can't come back to the court to change it or get a further amount later, there is scope for a later 'buy out' of a maintenance claim. Typically this happens when a husband has been ordered to pay his ex wife maintenance for the rest of her life. Later on, he accumulates enough capital to be able to offer a lump sum payment as a substitute for the maintenance. If this cannot be agreed between them, the court can order the payment, if it is satisfied that it is a reasonable amount to compensate the wife for the loss of her income.

Clean break order

This should include a provision to prevent each of you from having a claim on the estate of the other after death under the Inheritance (Provision for Family and Dependants) Act 1975.

DOING THE JUGGLE

So the process of arriving at the 'right' settlement for each couple is a juggle between resources, needs, and the ideas of fairness and compensation. The more you have, the greater the possibilities are. There are other things to bear in mind too. An asset may have one value on paper, but have an emotional value which it is hard to measure. You have to bear in mind the cost of dispute as it is possible to spend more on legal costs than the value of a particular asset.

Potential financial orders

When you are trying to work out a financial settlement you have to bear in mind the various orders that the court can make This section sets out the powers of the court and the usual ways in which such orders are made.

YOUR OPTIONS WITH THE HOME

For most families, what is to happen to the home is the first major decision to be faced. It doesn't matter whose name the house is in, or in what shares you hold it between you; the court can rearrange the shares or transfer the property between you. If you rent your home you may need to take special steps to protect your interest, so the court does have this power (see Chapter 7 'Emergencies').

Orders the court can make

- an order for maintenance 'pending suit' – which means before the decree absolute is granted.
- an order for periodical payments – often referred to as maintenance.
- an order for secured periodical payments.
- a lump-sum order.
- a property adjustment order.
- an order directing pension fund trustees to pay part or all of pension rights as they fall due.

An immediate sale

An immediate sale does not occur often, usually because one half of the couple wants to stay in the house and the assets can be sorted out so that this is possible. The problem with a sale is the amount you lose in paying estate agents and removal costs. If money is tight, as it is for most divorcing couples, this is a loss you want to avoid. If you are heavily in debt, you may have no choice and the house may have to be sold.

Divorce court orders

The orders that a divorce court can make about the family home:
- an immediate sale, with division of the proceeds.
- a postponed sale – usually until the children complete their education but sometimes beyond that, the house then to be sold and the proceeds divided in specified proportions.
- a transfer of one person's interest to the other with a lump-sum adjustment.
- outright transfer of one person's interest to the other.

Constructing an order for a postponed sale

This chart outlines the procedure for holding your property pending a sale.

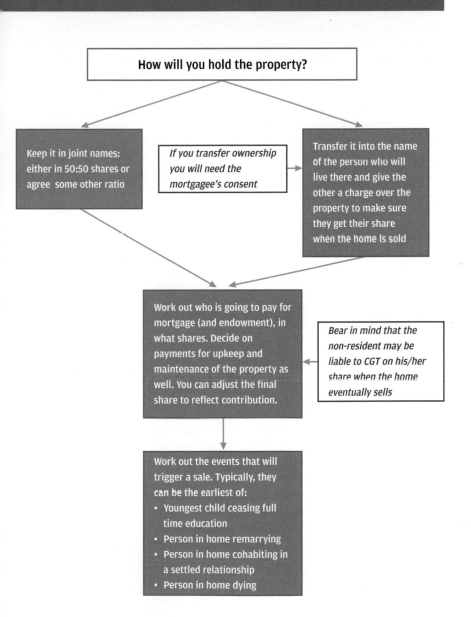

How will you hold the property?

Keep it in joint names: either in 50:50 shares or agree some other ratio

If you transfer ownership you will need the mortgagee's consent

Transfer it into the name of the person who will live there and give the other a charge over the property to make sure they get their share when the home is sold

Work out who is going to pay for mortgage (and endowment), in what shares. Decide on payments for upkeep and maintenance of the property as well. You can adjust the final share to reflect contribution.

Bear in mind that the non-resident may be liable to CGT on his/her share when the home eventually sells

Work out the events that will trigger a sale. Typically, they can be the earliest of:
- Youngest child ceasing full time education
- Person in home remarrying
- Person in home cohabiting in a settled relationship
- Person in home dying

Not selling immediately

If the house is your main asset, it may be fair that you both have a share of it. But an immediate sale may not make sense. This could be because the sale price is not good at present. There may be negative equity, so you still end up in debt after the sale, or you may have to pay back a Council discount. You may want to keep the home as the children's home for the time being. For any of these reasons (and others) you may feel that it is best to postpone the sale, but still keep your rights to a share of the proceeds when it is sold. There are various ways of arranging how you hold the property pending the sale (see chart on previous page).

Charge for the non-occupying person

If the home is in one person's name, the non-occupier protects his or her interest in the eventual proceeds of sale by having a 'charge' put on the property. This means that their interest is registered at the Land Registry on the title deeds so that anyone dealing with the property can see that they are entitled to a share in the proceeds of sale.

Selling later – pros and cons

Postponing a sale has its pitfalls, and there was a period when such orders attracted a certain amount of judicial disapproval because of this. The problems arise when the time comes for a sale. Typically the person who has left the home has, by this time, entered into another mortgage and bought another home. The lump sum that comes from the sale of the family home arrives as a bonus and helps to reduces his or her debts. However, there may be capital gains tax (CGT) to pay on the increase in value.

For the person who has stayed in the house, there are other difficulties. By the time the home is sold, the share of the home may not be enough to buy a new home outright. Postponing a sale also assumes that property prices will continue to rise; where they decline, it can leave the person who has stayed in the house in a difficult position when she/he has to find a new home. He or she is by this time several years older and may not find it so easy to raise a new mortgage. Even though he/she has known that one day the time will come when the sale must

---

 See Chapter 7 'Emergencies', about preventing the surrender of a tenancy.
For more information on Capital Gains Tax see www.hmrc.gov.uk/cgt/index.htm

happen, having to move is still difficult to face.

This is especially true when you see your ex secure in his or her new home. You need to make sure at the time of making the order that you do get a large enough share of the home to cover your future rehousing costs. You cannot go back to the court for a different order if things don't work out as you predicted.

The court does have power to order the occupier of the home to pay the other an occupation rent. This is very rarely invoked however, and would generally only be appropriate where there is no mortgage on the property.

Getting the consent of the mortgagee

If you are going to change the shares in which you hold the home, or transfer the home into one person's name, you will have to get the consent of the mortgagee (the bank or building society).

Although you can have a court order for the transfer of a property which is subject to a mortgage, the court has no power to order the bank or building society to agree. Without their consent the transfer can't go ahead so it is important that you have explored the idea with the mortgagee before you either agree a settlement or go to court.

Transferring to one person

If you are proposing to transfer the home into one person's name (with a charge to protect the other person's interest) then the mortgage will have to go into that sole person's name as well. This can cause problems if he or she

Case Study Ann and Mitch

Ann and Mitch split up and decided that Ann would stay in the home with their three children until it was sold. They then decided to divide the net proceeds of sale so that Ann would get 67%, and Mitch the rest (the house was in their joint names). They decided it would be best to transfer it into Ann's sole name so that Mitch could take out another mortgage on his new home – the building society said that they wouldn't give him a mortgage if he already had one. However, their existing building society said that Ann did not have enough income to take over the existing mortgage as it was more than two and a half times her salary. Ann was sure that she could manage to pay it with what she was getting in wages, tax credit and what Mitch was paying for the children. The Building Society would agree to the mortgage however if Mitch guaranteed the payments – which means he would have to pay them if Ann didn't. Mitch gave the guarantee, and Ann, in the court order, gave him an indemnity which said that she would reimburse him if he did have to pay the mortgage.

does not have enough income to meet the mortgagee's lending criteria. You may need to find another mortgagee or the non-occupier may need to guarantee the mortgage payments.

ENDOWMENT MORTGAGES

If you have an endowment mortgage you have an insurance policy linked to your mortgage. You pay interest on your mortgage each month, but you are not paying off any capital, so the amount that you owe the building society stays the same. You are also paying premiums on the insurance policy and (in theory) the value of the policy increases over time so that when the time comes to pay the mortgage off, the policy will be cashed in and pay it all.

However, endowment policies have had increasingly bad publicity over the last few years. Many of them have not increased enough in value. You may have heard from your mortgage company how financially healthy your particular endowment is; if not, contact the mortgage company.

SORTING OUT AN ENDOWMENT MORTGAGE

If you have an endowment mortgage, arrangements to transfer the home need to take account of the current value of the policy and the projected yield when it matures. If you intend to keep the policy with the mortgage, you must decide who is going to pay the premiums and who will have the benefit of the policy when it matures. You can transfer the policy into one person's name. Or you could cash it in. It is worth bearing in mind that you can also sell an endowment, and often get more for it than the insurance company will pay out if you cash it in early.

TRANSFERRING THE HOME WITH A LUMP SUM PAYMENT

If one of you has the money, or the mortgage raising capacity you may decide that he or she will buy the other person out of their share in the home. The mechanics of this in the court order are that one of you is ordered to transfer the home to the other and the other is ordered to make a lump sum payment. These two orders are to be complied with simultaneously.

TRANSFER OF ONE PERSON'S INTEREST TO THE OTHER

The court can also order, or you can agree, that one of you will transfer his/her interest in the home to the other. If there is a mortgage you will need the consent of the mortgagee, (the bank or building society). But in a contested hearing, the court cannot realistically make this order unless you have found out in advance that the mortgagee will consent to the transfer.

RENTED PROPERTY

A property transfer order can transfer the tenancy of most rented homes. If your spouse/cp, rather than you, is the tenant, you must ask the court for a transfer of tenancy order before the divorce decree is made absolute. This is because the occupation of the accommodation by the non-tenant spouse is keeping alive the protected, statutory, secure or assured tenancy arising from the 'deemed occupation' rules.

Once the marriage is ended on the final decree of divorce, these rules no longer apply, and the tenancy will lose its protected, secure or assured status, or, in the case of a statutory tenancy, will simply cease to exist. If a protected, statutory, secure or assured tenancy no longer exists, there is nothing for the court to transfer.

The general rule is that a transferee spouse cannot get better tenancy rights than the tenant spouse, so if the home is rented on a short-term basis the court will not be able to extend the term of the tenancy, and if rent payment debts have been built up then these would be passed on to the transferee. Although it is not often used, the court has the power to compensate the person transferring the tenancy by ordering the other person to make a payment.

Maintenance orders

There have recently been some highly publicised cases involving very rich couples where, wives who have contributed to their husbands' financial successes have been awarded maintenance at very high levels, over and above the samount of basic need.

This is, of course, only possible when incomes are very high. For most families, the starting point must be to look at what each person needs to live on. You then have to juggle this against the question of resources and see what can be afforded. If there is plenty of income, so that when reasonable needs are met there is still a surplus, then you would look at the reasoning in the House of Lords cases of Miller and Macfarlane. The court took into account what the wives in these cases had given up in terms of their careers because of their marriages.

MAINTENANCE PENDING SUIT (CP: 'PENDING OUTCOME')

This is maintenance that one spouse/cp can be ordered to pay to the other before the final decree is made. In most cases you can generally agree temporary maintenance while the divorce is ongoing. This can be put into a formal court order, but, in many cases, couples simply rely on the agreement and do not bother with the extra expense of making a court order.

Maintenance pending suit applications are comparatively infrequent because of the costs involved and the time taken up in the procedure.

PERIODICAL PAYMENTS (MAINTENANCE)

Generally, if there are any children, you look at their needs first and what can be afforded. After you have sorted that out, you consider whether there should be any maintenance for the adults. You must take into account the availability of tax credits and benefits in looking at the overall effect of any order.

For the children

Maintenance for children is generally expressed as an annual sum, to be paid weekly or monthly. If the order does not state that it is to be paid in advance, it is paid in arrears. The sum for each child should be stated. Maintenance will normally run until each child's

Children within the CSA	Children outside the CSA
If your children come within the jurisdiction of the CSA, then you can only make a court order by consent. Most parents will agree an amount, rather than use the CSA. You will generally use the CSA formula as a guideline. The court does have power to vary an order which was originally made by consent, so you can, later argue a change in the amount before the court.	Examples of these cases are: • children who are not yours by blood or adoption • children who are, or whose parent(s) are, habitually resident abroad (and not employed by a UK-based company) • disabled children who need more than the CSA formula provides The court can hear a contested application for their maintenance, if you cannot agree it.

seventeenth birthday, but the order can be worded to go on to the child's eighteenth birthday if he or she is expected to be still at school, or it can even continue until the child has ceased full-time education or training.

The court will generally use the CSA formula as a starting point, but there may be good reasons for departing from it, depending on the needs of the children and the resources available.

For the spouse/cp

Maintenance for a spouse/cp, as for children, is generally expressed as an annual sum, to be paid weekly or monthly. Occasionally, the court can specify that it is for life, in which case it will end on the death of either party; it will also end automatically on the remarriage of the recipient (but not his/her cohabitation) or if a court order terminates it.

A later court order can also vary the amount that must be paid (See 'Changes in circumstances: variations' on page 196).

Protecting the recipient of maintenance for life

If one person is going to have maintenance to last for the whole of her/his life (if she/he does not remarry) there is a potential problem if the payer dies first. The maintenance will then stop unless you make another arrangement. You can provide for this sometimes by adjusting the payer's pension arrangements, or it may be better to insure his or her life. The payer can take out a policy on his/her own life, or his/her ex can take out the policy, with the payer's cooperation. The amount insured needs to be calculated to meet the shortfall as far as possible. You need to decide who will be responsible for paying the premiums.

It is common for spousal maintenance to be ordered for a fixed period. The typical situation in which this would happen would be where a wife has had a period away from work to care for a young family but intends to return to work in a few years, or after a period of retraining. If maintenance is for a fixed period, the order can dismiss the wife's claims at the end of that period so that no further order can be made at all; or leave them open, which would give the opportunity for the order to be extended if unforeseen circumstances prevented the anticipated return to work.

 A secured order can only be made where there is a lot of available capital. As a result it is rarely made and should not be contemplated without legal advice.

 Payment guidelines
There are no set guidelines on how much maintenance should be paid for spouses/CPs.

SECURED PAYMENTS

If the court makes a maintenance order in circumstances where it seems highly likely that payments will not be made, the court has the power to order that periodical payments be 'secured' by a capital asset possessed by the paying party. This means that the asset can be sold to provide the money if payments are not made. The court can also make this order if the payments are not made subsequently and other methods of enforcement cannot be used.

Capital orders

When the court looks at capital orders – lump sum, transfer of property and pension adjustment – it first has to consider the available resources, and how they can be sensibly divided up.

It is unlikely, for example, that a court would order the sale of a small family company simply in order to divide the proceeds, because it might make better economic sense to keep it as a going concern. In addition to the needs and resources of both parties, what the individuals have contributed to the marriage is also taken into account.

LUMP SUM

A lump sum order is a capital order. One of you can be ordered to pay the other a lump sum, either all at once or by specified instalments. The date by which the payment(s) should be made should be in the order. The order can provide for interest to be paid if the payment is late.

In addition to any final order that the court might make, it can make a lump sum order at a later stage if a periodical payments order is ended by a court order. This can be a useful way of creating a clean break between husband and wife where this was not possible at the time of the divorce.

TRANSFER OF PROPERTY ORDER

A transfer of property order generally involves the transfer of the family home between the couple, but 'property' is defined widely and can include other items such as a council tenancy, or shares, and not just what lawyers call 'real' property (houses or land).

The court can order one of you to transfer property to the other, or adjust the proportion of the property each of you owns. It can order the sale of a property and the shares in which the proceeds are to be divided. It cannot order a third party to make a transfer, nor, as we have described, can it order a mortgagee – the building society or the bank – to cooperate in the transfer.

Pension rights

There has been increasing concern about women being potential losers over pensions when their marriage breaks up. This is particularly the case if:

- The wife has spent her time largely looking after the children and home and has either no, or relatively low, earnings from which to make her own savings for retirement; or
- A more mature wife, who fully expected to share in the benefits of her husband's pension, and again has devoted herself to children and the home, finds she is divorced and will have insufficient time to build up a reasonable pension, even if she were able to get a job of her own.

> **!** **Payment guidelines**
> Pensions present complex legal and mathematical problems and you need good legal advice on these issues.

OFFSETTING

In general, offsetting, that is, giving one spouse/cp a greater share of the family home or a larger lump-sum payment in recognition of the loss of her or his pension rights, is preferred to earmarking (see below) by the court. Earmarking is only used when no assets are available to offset.

Two considerations are likely to reduce any payment made. The first is the fact that the receiving spouse/cp will be getting a certain amount right away, and will therefore not be subject to uncertainties about the performance of the funds invested or whether the pension member might die before retirement or soon after.

Second, the lump sum or assets transferred (often the family home) is likely to be tax free (whereas earmarked pension payments will bear income tax on current rates of between 0 and 40 per cent).

EARMARKING

The court can order pension trustees or managers to 'earmark' part of the pension to be paid at retirement to an ex: in other words, to allocate a share of the pension (and any tax-free cash taken at retirement) to the ex for the future. (The courts can also order part of a lump sum payable on death to be paid to the ex.)

The part which is earmarked can either be a percentage of the whole pension or a fixed sum. Once it starts to be paid – on retirement – the earmarked pension will be paid directly from the pension scheme to the ex. The court can specifically make the pension trustees pay up, overriding their discretion.

PENSION SHARING

The court has a further option: pension sharing. Pension sharing has proved more popular than ear-marking. This is because the ex's rights to a pension are not dependent on uncontrollable factors, such as a husband's premature death. Also, pension sharing makes a clean break between the spouses. A court cannot make an order to 'earmark' and 'share' the same pension. You cannot, for instance, have an order earmarking a share in the lump-

sum death-in-service benefit and share other rights.

The pension scheme managers or trustees can make reasonable charges for the costs involved in administering a pension-sharing order. The National Association of Pension Funds recommends £750 to £1,000 +VAT per case. The costs involved in valuations and administration mean that in cases where the pension rights are small, it is probably much more sensible to look at compensating a spouse rather than sharing the pension fund.

The court can direct that a very wide range of pension rights be shared, including any SERPS and S2P pensions (see Appendix... for details), additional voluntary contributions and contracted-out pension rights. However, pension sharing cannot apply to the state basic pension (which is already subject to special rules on divorce), state graduated pension, widow's and widower's pensions or a lump-sum death benefit. There is no automatic 50:50 split – each case is determined (or settled) on its merits. In theory the court could order, say, a 10:90 split

In Scotland, pension sharing can be effected simply by agreement between the parties. In England and Wales it must be by court order, though this can be a consent order.

Under pension sharing, the value of the pension holder's rights is calculated using the cash equivalent transfer rate (CETV) method (see Pension valuations, below). Part of that value is then transferred to the other spouse/cp to fund her/his own pension. The value of the pension holder's rights is reduced by the sum transferred.

In England and Wales, the amount transferred is a given percentage of the CETV. In Scotland, the amount transferred may be a percentage or alternatively a specified cash sum. Another difference is that in Scotland only pension rights built up while the couple were married are considered. In England and Wales this limit does not apply, so rights built up before marriage can be taken into account if appropriate.

There are two types of transfer that the court can order. (See box). If the pension holder works in the public sector, usually only an internal transfer will be allowed. This is because many public-sector pension schemes – for example, for the police, civil servants and teachers – are unfunded, which means that any payments out of them are met using taxpayers' money. The government was reluctant to risk an immediate tax burden caused by transfer payments from these schemes, so it drew up the rules to prohibit external transfers in the case of unfunded public-sector schemes. Where (less commonly) a public-sector scheme is funded – for example, the local authority superannuation scheme – external transfers must be offered. Where the pension holder is a member of a private-sector scheme which is funded (as is normally the case), external transfers must be offered and internal transfers may be available. An unfunded private-sector scheme does not have to offer external transfers.

VALUING A PENSION

The various regulations that govern pensions in divorce settlements say that you should take the CETV (Cash Equivalent Transfer Value) of the pension as the figure that you use for calculating its value. This is the lump sum which, if invested now, might be expected to provide enough cash by retirement to buy the pension.

However pensions experts advise that this valuation method can undershoot the real value because it crystallises the value of your pension rights now, ignoring how they would have changed in the remaining time until retirement. With a salary-related pension the CETV ignores future increases in earnings, and with a money-purchase pension, hefty transfer charges might be deducted. This means that CETV tends to favour the person giving up the pension rights and short-changes the person being compensated or given a share of the rights.

Pension schemes can produce a CETV fairly simply. A fee for preparing the valuation by the pension trustees or managers will have to be paid by the pension-scheme holder (or sometimes the spouse), the amount is likely to be set by each individual plan. With the court's permission and the agreement of the parties involved, an alternative to CETV can be used to value the pension rights if that would be more appropriate.
Once the basic information about the pension is available, if the

pension is potentially valuable, solicitors will often advise their client to instruct an actuary to prepare a valuation. Pension valuations can be prepared from instructions given jointly by the husband's and wife's solicitors.

What orders you can have about pensions

- giving one of you a bigger share of other assets to offset your loss of her interest in your spouse/cp's pension
- giving one of you a lump sum to compensate you for the loss of specific benefits, such as the right to receive a widow's pension
- earmarking part or all of a future lump sum payable on death of one of you for payment to your ex
- requiring one of you swap part of the pension for a lump sum at retirement (called 'commutation') and earmarking part or all of that lump sum to the ex
- earmarking part of your pension (either a future pension or one currently being received) to be paid to your ex (only in England and Wales, not in Scotland)
- 'pension sharing' – in other words, transferring part of one person's pension rights to the other.

For pension valuations: The Divorce Corporation, 187 Baslow Rd, Sheffield, S17 4DT, Tel: 0114-262 0616, Fax: 0114 235 0878, e-mail divorce_corporation@btconnect.com, Society of Pension Consultants, St Bartholomew House, 92 Fleet Street, London EC4Y 1DG, Tel: 020-7353 1688, Fax: 020-7353 9296, www.spc.uk.com

THINGS THE COURT CANNOT ORDER BUT YOU CAN PUT IN A CONSENT ORDER

The court has a limited repertoire of orders. If you can agree a settlement together, you can extend this by making binding promises ('undertakings') to each other. These are enforceable.

You can also agree about things that a court order does not generally need to cover, such as what will happen to the contents of the home. These are seldom worth very much at market value, as they are second hand, but they obviously have a very great importance for you and the children. You can state that you do not intend to make any claims over anything else that you each own. You can declare that you will both not use the CSA unless you are obliged to.

All of these extra promises and declarations enable you to make an order which can be much more detailed than a contested court ruling. You can also trade obligations and thus feel that you have made a better bargain with each other.

List of promises that you might make to each other

- to pay off debts, such as credit cards
- to buy (and insure) a car
- to obtain a Get (Jewish bill of divorce)
- maintain medical insurance cover
- leave items by will
- cooperate in the taking out of life insurance
- not to disclose information (to the press, for instance)
- to resign as a director
- do your best to get the other person released from a mortgage

 For pension valuations: Association of Consulting Actuaries, Warnford Court, 29 Throgmorton Street, London, EC2N 2AT, Tel: 020 7382 4594, Fax: 020 7374 6220, Email: acahelp@aca.org.uk, www.aca.org.uk

Applying to the court for an order

Even if you agree everything about the finances between you, you will still need a court order, though one made by consent. This section tells you how the court procedure works

Many couples start out with some disagreements and you may need to go part of the way down the route of a contested application before you can settle the case.

PERFECT TIMING

Sorting out your finances in a divorce is a separate matter from the divorce proceedings themselves. However, the timings have to coincide at some points. You cannot actually file a financial application until the divorce petition has been filed (though this does not stop you starting to negotiate about finances). A final financial order cannot be made by the court until decree nisi, but often the terms of such an order are agreed before decree nisi and

Final orders
The rules about when final orders can be made do not stop interim orders for maintenance or maintenance pending suit orders being made if necessary pending decree absolute.

submitted to the court for approval at the same time as the decree. The final financial order cannot actually take effect until decree absolute, the final decree of divorce. The order may well come some time after the decree absolute, so that you can be divorced and free to remarry but not have your financial situation sorted out.

FINANCIAL APPLICATIONS

You can sort out the financial issues between you at any stage. Sometimes these are sorted out with relative ease and no financial applications are filed: a consent order is simply submitted for the court's approval. More often, a

> ❝ Only a small percentage of cases go all the way to the final hearing. ❞

financial application will be filed and proceed to a greater or lesser extent before both of you feel comfortable enough with the information that you have obtained about each other's finances to be able to settle. Sometimes such settlement is not reached until the very day of the final hearing, 'at the court door'. Perhaps surprisingly, given the way that these things are reported in the press, only a very small percentage of cases actually end up before a district judge who has to decide how the assets are to be divided. The court takes more control over the progress of the financial application than it does in the divorce. There is a strict timetable for the progress of cases. The court also keeps a close eye on the level of costs so that they do not escalate unreasonably. You are encouraged, even obliged, to be frank about your negotiating positions, rather than play cat and mouse. For the same reason, simultaneous exchange of information is prescribed; the content and format of the initial exchange of information is also laid down.

The judge in a case will try to mediate a solution, or may refer the couple to mediation.

" The parties themselves can decide at any point to settle the matter. "

Making the application

This section sets out the court procedure you have to follow when you make an application for a financial order. Full details are supplied below as to which forms you will need to complete and where you can obtain the necessary paperwork.

THE APPLICATION FORM

If you want to apply to the court for an order, you start by filling in a Form A which is available from the court or the Courts Service website and filing it (and two copies of it) at the court where the divorce proceedings are taking place. The fee is £210 (the usual exemptions apply). The form simply notifies the court and your spouse/cp that you intend to proceed with the financial application.

You do not have to file evidence of your financial position at the time that you make the application. This comes later (see below).

It is important to bear in mind that once you have filed Form A you are on a tight timescale, with which you must comply. It would be prudent to make sure that you are going to be able to get together all the financial evidence that you need in time before you start.

Filling in Form A

You tick boxes to show which of the orders you intend to apply for:

- an order for maintenance pending suit
- a periodical payments order
- a secured provision order
- a lump sum order
- a property adjustment order
- a pension sharing/attachment order.

If you intend to make an application for periodical payments for the children, you have to tick boxes to show why the court has jurisdiction and the CSA does not.

THE 'FIRST APPOINTMENT'

Once the court receives Form A it will fix what is officially known as

Go to the Courts Service website for details of the forms you need to apply for an order: www.hmcourts-service.gov.uk

Ancillary relief procedure

Follow these steps to see how a final order is ma

Applicant files
Form A

↓

Court fixes date
for first
appointment

5 weeks before date
couple must exchange Form E;
15 days before it, other
documentation must be
exchanged

12 to 16 weeks later

↓

First Appointment

Judge can make,
or couple can
agree, a final order

If no final order
possible judge will
give directions for
further
information for
FDR appointment

Judge can also
send couple to
mediation

↓

FDR Appointment

Judge can make,
or couple can
agree, a final order

If no final order
possible judge will
give directions for
further information
for final hearing

↓

Final Hearing

Negotiations to settle
the case can take place at any
time before or during the
proceedings

Judge makes, or
couple can agree,
final order

a First Appointment. This must take place between 12 and 16 weeks from the date on which you filed Form A. The court will not change the date for any trivial reason, and it can be changed only with the court's permission or with the consent of your spouse/cp.

Before the first appointment

At least five weeks (35 days) before the First Appointment, you must exchange with your spouse/cp full details of your financial position on Form E. This form is extremely detailed, and it must be completed thoroughly. (See page 188, on disclosure.) You, or your solicitor, will need to contact your spouse/cp, or his or her solicitor, to agree the date on which the forms are to be exchanged. Depending on the date on which the court fixes the First Appointment, you will have between seven and eleven weeks to complete Form E. This may seem a long time, but the detail that the form requires means that it is going to be quite a task unless your financial position is very straightforward. If you are the applicant, it makes sense to start compiling the information as soon as possible. If you think that your spouse/cp is going to be an applicant, you should also be putting the information together as soon as you can. It will save you

solicitors' time and costs if you can do much of this yourself.

Form E has to be sworn (like an affidavit) and filed at court, as well as being served on your spouse/cp.

At least two weeks (14 days) before the First Appointment, other documents must be filed and served on your spouse/cp.

WHAT HAPPENS AT THE FIRST APPOINTMENT

You and your spouse/cp have to attend the court. If you have solicitors, they will be there too. If you do not attend, you can be penalised in costs.

At the First Appointment the judge may take the view that there is a need for further information to be provided by one or both of you, and will make orders ('directions') about what needs to be filed and when the next hearing will be. If enough information has been filed and you and your spouse/cp are in a position to agree a settlement, a final order can be made. If financial issues cannot be sorted out in this way, the judge can either adjourn the case so that you can go to mediation, or refer the case to an FDR appointment.

FINANCIAL DISPUTE RESOLUTION (FDR)

Both of you should attend (unless the judge orders otherwise) the FDR appointment. The hearing is described as 'informal', which means that the judge can run it as he or she thinks best. Each judge will have a slightly different style of dealing with the matter, so it is impossible to describe exactly what will happen. It is intended that the appointment will give an opportunity for negotiation and discussion. The judge will attempt to find a settlement that both of you feel you can agree to.

At least seven days before the hearing, the applicant must file at the court a bundle of all offers and proposals that have been made or received by either party; this applies whether the offers were made 'without prejudice' or not. If the case does not resolve at the FDR, this bundle will not be shown to the judge at the final hearing, who will in any case be a different judge from the one who conducted the FDR. This means that the 'privileged' aspect of 'without prejudice' correspondence is preserved.

COSTS DISCLOSURE

The rules require both of you to come to each hearing with a statement of the costs that you have incurred so far. This has to be filled in on Form H. The court will expect the costs to be 'proportionate' to the issues in the case.

DISCLOSURE

It is a fundamental principle in dealing with financial matters that both the couple should give 'full and frank disclosure' of their individual financial positions, supplying documentary proof where appropriate.

Form E

Disclosure of financial matters is controlled by the court rules. Form E lays down what information should be filed (see box opposite). The form should have documents supplied with it to back up the information. You can attach any other documents that explain or clarify any information given on the form.

Documents to go with Form E

Documents to go with Form E include:
- a valuation of the family home (if obtained in the last 12 months)
- a copy of your most recent mortgage statement
- bank statements for all your accounts for the last 12 months
- surrender-value quotations for any life policies
- if you have a business, accounts for the last two years and any other document that supports a valuation
- last three payslips and most recent P60
- if you are in a partnership, accounts for the last two accounting years.

QUESTIONNAIRES

Once you have read your spouse/cp's Form E you may feel that he or she should provide more information about his or her assets. You can send a questionnaire to elicit this information. However, instead of sending it simply to your spouse/cp, it has to be filed at the court, and you have to notify the court that you want to do this, at least two weeks before the First Appointment (as described above). If you do not feel the need for a questionnaire, you have to state that you are not going to use one.

Because of the tight timescale you may have only five weeks to draw up a questionnaire or decide that you do not want one, if you

have exchanged Form E at the last possible date.

FURTHER DISCLOSURE

No further evidence of finances can be filed or sought without the leave of the court. The implication of the rules is that it will be hard to get leave unless you can make out a convincing case that information has been withheld and that it will make a material difference to the outcome of the case.

EXPERT EVIDENCE

Occasionally you may need the evidence of a third party before the court. If this is an expert, such as a valuer, the court will give directions on this and if possible both of you should instruct the expert. This is to prevent each of you producing partisan witnesses whose fees will increase the overall costs.

THIRD PARTIES

You may feel that it is important to get evidence from a third party – the most likely situation is where you want to find out about the finances of your spouse/cp's new partner. Your spouse/cp cannot be compelled to produce evidence about him or her, and in any case may claim not to know any details. The other person cannot be compelled by the court to file a Form E, because he or she is not a party to the proceedings. But the court does have power to require a third party to attend the court with documents, which can then be inspected. To obtain such an 'inspection appointment', you have to file an affidavit explaining what documents you want to see and why they are relevant to the case. It is then for the judge to decide whether it would be appropriate to order the attendance of the third party.

THE FINAL HEARING

If you are unable to resolve the case at the First Appointment, the FDR appointment, or by negotiation as the case goes on, then the matter will come to a final hearing. This will be, like the other appointments, in private – 'in chambers', as lawyers sometimes say.

You both have to go into the final hearing having 'shown your hand' about the orders that you want the court to make. You have to file at court and serve on your spouse a statement that sets out, with the details of the amounts involved, the orders that you want the court to make for you. If it was your application in the first place, you have to file and serve this statement at least 14 days before the hearing. The respondent has to file his or her statement within seven days of receiving yours.

At the hearing both of you will have an opportunity to state your case, either in person or through your solicitor or barrister. Either of you may be asked to give evidence on oath, if only to bring the financial disclosure up to date. The convention is that the applicant gives evidence first and can then be cross-examined. Then the other party gives evidence and can be cross-examined, if appropriate.

Tips on giving oral evidence

- always listen carefully to any questions put to you and answer clearly
- remember that the person whom you need to convince is the judge, not the lawyers.
- speak slowly: often the other party's solicitor and the judge (as well as your solicitor, if instructed) will be taking notes of what you are saying.
- avoid becoming heated or emotional in response to the other party's questions; the judge will want to confine his or her enquiry to the facts.

Negotiating a financial settlement

You may be relieved to know that only a small percentage – about 10 per cent – of divorce cases end up in a full-blown battle over money. This section will help to guide you through the procedures involved in the financial settlement.

The majority of divorce cases are settled by agreement at some stage along the line: at the very beginning of the separation (or before), or even on the steps outside the court doors just before the final financial hearing is to be held. The fact that mediation is now more widely available and can be used by families who want to save on legal costs also offers another option to resolve family disputes speedily, efficiently and effectively.

Advantages of an agreement

Whenever an agreement is made, the family as a whole is likely to save significantly on legal costs. There are rare cases where a spouse/cp pretends to make an agreement while in reality he or she is determined to drag out the process of resolution, but as a general rule making agreements will save you money, and the earlier you can do so the more money will be saved on legal fees.

CONSENT ORDERS

Although you have the option of keeping your agreements oral and relying on your spouse/cp's sense of honour, the problem is that such agreements have a habit of unravelling over time, as one or other of you claims no longer to be able to 'remember' the terms. So, to protect yourself properly, an agreement should be drawn up in the form of a separation agreement or deed or, better still, a consent order made by the court. If you have reached a settlement through mediation, this will usually be drawn up in the form of a 'Summary' or 'Memorandum of Understanding'. This again should be translated, usually by solicitors, into a court order which you seek from the court to make the settlement financially watertight.

PROPOSALS

Once you are satisfied that you have a clear view of the overall financial picture and that both of you have fully disclosed your financial positions to each other, you can put forward proposals for settlement on a 'without prejudice' basis. This means that if the proposals do not result in settlement and litigation does follow, they cannot be referred to in a final hearing before a court (as described earlier, they must be disclosed to the FDR appointment judge). Any 'open' negotiation (as opposed to one that is 'without prejudice') that you have, or your solicitor has, with your spouse would place you in a vulnerable position, in that your spouse/cp could later use in court any admissions you have made. Accordingly, if your solicitor is conducting negotiations for you, he or she will automatically head proposals with the words 'without prejudice'; if you are conducting negotiations yourself, you should do the same.

Usually it is the spouse/cp who will be paying maintenance and/or a lump sum who puts forward the first proposals; frequently (but not always) these result in counter-proposals from the other. Generally, the eventual agreement will fall somewhere between these two sets of proposals.

FINANCIAL AGREEMENTS AND DIVORCE

If couples agree a financial order, rather than have one decided by the court, it is known as a 'consent order'. An application for a consent order involves drawing up the draft court order that you would like the court to make: this is usually called by lawyers 'minutes of agreement and consent order' or 'minutes of order'. This too can be tailor-made to fit your own requirements (and so can often suit an individual family far better than can a court order made by the court after a battle).

One of the main reasons why lawyers emphasise that a court order should be drawn up, instead of leaving an oral or written agreement as it stands, is the issue of a clean break. You may have amicably agreed to a clean break: that you will divide your assets to give one of you a greater share to compensate her or him for giving up claims for maintenance. But so long as no court has formally ordered a dismissal of the maintenance claims, they can still be activated at a later stage. If circumstances changed you would still be able to make a further claim for maintenance (unless you

 To ensure that the form of a proposed consent order is as watertight, tax efficient and comprehensive as possible, you should instruct a solicitor to draw up the documents.

had remarried). Capital claims that have been listed in the 'prayer' of the continue, even after remarriage, unless dismissed by the court.

Note that making a clean-break order by consent will not preclude a future application for child support via the CSA. You cannot have a clean break as far as the children are concerned.

DRAWING UP A CONSENT ORDER

A minutes of order typically starts with an outline of the basis of the agreement. Then it contains undertakings: solemn and binding promises that you make to each other. These can cover aspects of the settlement that the court cannot formally order, such as a promise by one of you to provide medical insurance for the children. The formal orders follow, and should include everything that has been agreed including any agreement about costs.

At any time within the divorce proceedings you can apply for a consent order for maintenance pending suit (temporary maintenance payments made to a spouse until the decree absolute) and for interim periodical payments for children.

For a final consent order (lump-sum, property adjustment or periodical payments) you cannot apply until you apply for 'directions for trial' under the special procedure. The order will not be made until the decree nisi has been pronounced and will not become effective until decree absolute.

The fee for a consent order application is £40.

MAKING OF THE CONSENT ORDER

Once the consent order minutes, financial statement and applications have been lodged at the court, the district judge will review them. Provided the district judge has sufficient information to be satisfied that the proposed terms are reasonable and both parties are in agreement, he or she is likely to accept the agreement and issue a formal consent order as requested.

If the agreement is put forward by solicitors on each side, the district judge may approve it without either of you having to attend in person, but if you are acting for yourself, the district judge will probably make an appointment to discuss the proposed order with you and your spouse/cp, and may require further evidence, especially if no Form E has been filed. Approval by a district judge is not a rubber-stamping procedure: in certain cases, where the district judge feels that the order is unfair to either party, he or she may refuse to make it (although, again, this is unlikely if you have negotiated terms through a solicitor).

EFFECT OF A CONSENT ORDER

Consent orders, once made, are as effective as orders made by the court after a full hearing. The undertakings can be enforced as well as the actual orders. You cannot appeal a consent order, because that would be logically impossible. You can however apply to have it 'set aside' but only on limited grounds of:

- fresh evidence that could not have been known at the time
- fundamental mistakes, such as wholly erroneous information, on which all parties, including the court, relied
- fraud (which may include evidence that the other party had no intention of ever abiding by the terms of the order)
- lack of full and frank disclosure, if such disclosure would have resulted in an order substantially different from that which was made
- in certain rare circumstances, where the fundamental basis on which the order was made has been destroyed.

What to do with your court order

If you are acting for yourself, the court will send the court order to you. If you have a solicitor, he or she will be sent the copy and will send it on to you. However, there are several key considerations you need to be aware of.

CHECK IT

The first thing to do is check it through carefully. Sometimes errors creep in even if the order was made by consent. If there is anything that is the result of a typing or transcribing error, the court can put it right under what is called the 'slip rule'. If there is anything that you do not understand in the order (with a consent order this is unlikely to happen because you should have seen it before it went to the court), you should discuss it with your solicitor straight away – or go back to the court if you are acting for yourself.

MAKE SURE THE ORDER IS CARRIED OUT

You need to make sure that you keep to any promises that you have made or things that you have been ordered to do. There may be time limits that you need to keep to. You do not want to find yourself in breach of the order simply because you have overlooked part of it. Also, you need to check that your ex keeps to his or her part of the order. It is important to realise that

❝ The longer maintenance remains unpaid, the harder it is to recover, so it is important to be alert at this stage. ❞

no one else polices the order for you; the court does not have any supervisory role, and your solicitor will not get involved in the implementation of the order unless there is something legal to be done, like the transfer of the home. Arrears of maintenance can quickly build up after an order is made unless the payer makes immediate arrangements and the payee makes sure that payments are made on the correct dates.

Keep the order safe

You must keep the order safe. It would be a good idea to take a photocopy and put the court copy away securely. Some orders have a long-term effect such as orders where the sale of the home is postponed until the children grow up.

After the order

You may need to vary or enforce an order once it has been put into effect. This section will show you the range of different factors that you might need to consider when and if you have to do this.

APPEALS

An appeal against an order or decision of the district judge can be made to a judge by filing a notice of appeal within 14 days. The fee for this is £100. The notice setting out the grounds for an appeal is best prepared by a solicitor.

ENFORCEMENT OF PAYMENTS

Whether you actually receive maintenance following a court order or CSA assessment often depends on the continuing ability of your ex to make the payments. Should the payer fall into arrears with maintenance payments, there are several channels for enforcement, none entirely satisfactory. The sooner steps are taken to enforce the arrears, the better. If arrears are allowed to accumulate, they may prove impossible to recover: courts will not generally enforce arrears that are more than a year old. The Chart on pages 198–9 sets out the main enforcement procedures that you can use.

DISAPPEARING EX

If you do not know your ex's address, it may be possible to get the DWP to disclose it to the court because the address may be known to it through National Insurance records. You can get a form from the court on which you should give as much information as you can about your ex's last known address and employer, date of birth and National Insurance number.

VARIATION OF ORDERS

After an order has been made circumstances may change. As a result, the original order may need changing too (see box opposite).

Only some orders can be varied. Transfer of property and lump sum orders cannot be changed, except for a lump sum payable by instalments; the court can change the timing, though not the overall sum. Maintenance orders can be changed, and so can deferred pension attachment lump sums. If the original maintenance order was for a fixed period, you can apply to

Typical reasons for an application for a variation

- a change in financial circumstances of the payer or payee, including retirement
- remarriage of the payee (a periodical payments order ends automatically, so normally no application is necessary)
- cohabitation of the payee
- remarriage or cohabitation of the payer
- death of either
- either becoming disabled
- children becoming significantly older
- length of time elapsed since the making of the last order.

Varying CSA maintenance

There is an inbuilt review every two years. Parents are asked to an update of their finances and maintenance is reassessed.

If you have a change in circumstances either of you can ask for a review but the review will not be made if the change is to the non-resident parent's income and the change is not more than 5 per cent (up or down).

extend it, if you apply before the term runs out.

RETIREMENT

In the case of either the recipient's or the payer's retirement, an application can be made to vary a maintenance order if one of you is feeling the pinch. Usually, the court will look at the actual needs and resources of the parties and will be concerned to try to share out the more limited finances fairly. There are, however, extra tax allowances available for those over 65 which could help financially.

Varying an order in the divorce proceedings

Relevant law	Matrimonial Causes Act 1973 s.31	Civil Partnership Act 2004 Schedule 5 Part 11
What the court must consider	All the circumstances, with particular regard to the children's welfare and any changes in the factors that were relevant when the original order was made.	
What the court can do	• Change the amount to be paid, up or down • Extend or reduce the length of time over which the payments are to be made • Substitute a lump sum for a spouse/cp's maintenance	
How do you apply	In the same way as you apply for an original financial order in the divorce proceedings. The fee is £210.	

Enforcing a court order

Payments of maintenance.

Need permission from court if arrears are over 12 months old.

Lump sum payments

CSA maintenance	Attachments of earnings order	Registration in Magistrates' Court
With a CSA assessment, the CSA will apply their own enforcement procedures. Poor reputation for efficiency	If payer is employed court can order employer to deduct payments direct from wages. Court may reassess amount.	Once this happens the court can enforce the order, by attachment, seizure of goods or committal to prison. Court can reassess amount
	Form: N337 Fee: £65 Affidavit setting out the debt	Form : M33 Fee: £35 Certified copy of the order

Information leaflet from the Courts Service	EX323

Property transfer

Warrant of execution	Committal by way of judgement summons	Charging order
Court instructs bailiff to seize goods which can be sold to produce the amount owed. Only worth doing if there are enough assets. County Court up to £5,000; if more transfer to High Court	If you prove payer has means to pay the court can order him/her to be committed to prison for up to six weeks if doesn't pay.	The court can impose a charge on the debtor's property and, if the debt is not paid, order the sale. Court can execute the sale document if debtor does not cooperate
Form N323 Fee: £55 if debt over £125 Affidavit setting out the debt	Form: M16 Fee: £95 Affidavit setting out the debt and the means to pay	Form: N379 Fee: £55 Affidavit setting out the details
EX322		EX325

What happens if the ex getting the maintenance...

Remarries	Cohabits	Dies
Her or his right to maintenance ceases immediately and cannot be revived against the ex-spouse/cp even if she or he is subsequently divorced, separated or widowed. If you go on taking the maintenance you can be made to pay it back.	Rights to maintenance do not end, but there might be grounds for asking for a variation. The court won't automatically treat new partner as having an obligation to support.	Maintenance stops.

Children's maintenance is not affected

What happens if the ex paying the maintenance...

Remarries	Cohabits	Dies
He or she may be able to apply for a variation but the court will treat the claims of the first spouse/cp as taking precedence over the new partner.		Maintenance stops, unless it has been secured. The recipient may be able to claim against the estate unless claims have already been dismissed in the divorce proceedings

Cohabiting couples

There are no rules to tell you how to organise your split, nor any rules that say that either of you must make a payment to the other, of income or capital. Proposals to change the law to give cohabitants more rights are still at an early stage. This chapter sets out the limited law that is available to help you, and this applies equally to male-female and same-sex couples.

PART 3

10

Splitting up

If you stop living together this has very limited legal implications. This is because the law only recognises your living together in a few areas. A break-up will mainly affect any tax credits or benefits that either of you claim.

You will need to tell the benefits office and the HMRC that you are no longer living together. If you have children, then you should read Chapter 6 about children's maintenance.

It is possible to be separated but still live under the same roof. From a legal point of view this needs to be more than just the ending of a sexual relationship. You would need to run two separate households, with separate finances, cooking, eating and cleaning arrangements.

SORTING OUT YOUR FINANCES

If you have already made a 'Living Together Agreement' this may have (indeed, should have) set out what you promised to do about money if you split up. If the agreement was in the form of a deed, it is legally enforceable and you can choose to stand by it and enforce it if your partner defaults. If you have not made an agreement, then you will have to rely on the very limited amount of law.

MAINTENANCE

There is no obligation in law for cohabitants to pay maintenance to each other. Only your children have maintenance rights (see Chapter 6).

However, the court cannot 'tuck in' extra maintenance for you if you are the parent with whom they live. The only way in which you could get maintenance would be if your former partner were prepared to pay

 There is no mechanism in the law for one former cohabitant to claim maintenance from the other for him or herself under any circumstances.

 For further reading on Living Together Agreements www.advicenow.org.uk and follow links to the living together pages.

it to you voluntarily. As there is no way in which you could compel him/her to make this payment, you will be relying on his or her generosity,, or you might be able to agree it as part of a deal, in return for a share of capital that he or she would otherwise not have any entitlement to.

If you can make such an agreement, you could record it in a legal deed and, if properly drawn up, could be enforceable in a court. That is not because of the maintenance element, but because of the form of the deed which creates an enforceable contract between you. If you do decide to do this, then you

“ There is a popular belief that if you have lived together for a particular period of time (two years is often quoted) you get maintenance rights but this is not the case. ”

need to take legal advice to get the agreement properly drawn up.

If you had a living together agreement that was drawn up as a deed and includes a promise to pay maintenance if you split up, then this, too, should be enforceable.

SORTING OUT THE FAMILY HOME

If you made a living together agreement with/or a declaration of trust in your home and you are happy to abide by your original agreement about the division of the home, then you will have saved yourself a great deal of time and legal costs and you can happily ignore the rest of this chapter.

The rights of cohabitants to the home in which they have lived together are not clear cut. There is no convenient Act that sets out the law or regulates your rights and duties to each other. Instead, there are a number of Acts which have some bearing on the legal problem, there are numerous cases, each of which hinges on its own facts, and there is

---

Maintenance agreements

When you are thinking about what should go into a maintenance agreement you need to include:

- clear details of the amount
- whether it is to be paid weekly or monthly or at another interval
- how it is to be paid (cheque/cash/standing order)
- whether it is to be paid in arrears or advance
- whether it is to be increased and if so by how much
- What events might cause it to end (death/marriage/another cohabitation)

If you are not specific, it can be hard to enforce an agreement even if it has been made as a deed.

---

what lawyers call common law and equity – the principles of law that have evolved over centuries. Through all this you and your lawyers will have to pick your way. This chapter may therefore seem confusing but we can only hope to provide an outline of the principles that the law will apply, and stress that for this you will probably need good legal advice.

There are different considerations that apply to your home depending on whether you own or rent it. (See chart on page 209.)

A HOME THAT YOU OWN

This section deals with property that you own, whether jointly, or in one person's name. Again, there are different legal positions, depending whether you own the home jointly or in one person's name.

Jointly held property

There are two ways of owning a property jointly and it is important to find out which one applies to you.

The two legal terms are 'joint tenancy' and 'tenancy in common'.

When you bought the home jointly, or transferred it from one of you to both of you, you should have been advised of the legal implications and a declaration of trust should have been drawn up. If your solicitor did not do this, you may have the basis for a claim against the firm See box opposite.

You may have had a formal declaration of trust to establish the shares in which you hold the home. You may have had some other sort of written agreement; a letter from one of you to the other might be enough. Or you can have had a verbal agreement. However, a verbal agreement, or even a loosely written one, can be problematic as very often there will be a difference between your two recollections of what was originally agreed.

If you are both certain about the terms of your agreement you would expect to be bound by it. However

---

Jargon buster

Joint tenancy: Under a joint tenancy, each person's interest in the property is not quantified: you own the whole of the house (or flat) jointly. When one of you dies, the whole property automatically passes to the survivor, irrespective of any provision the former may have made in a will. The law assumes a 50:50 split.

Tenancy in common: Under a tenancy in common, on the other hand, the interests of each person are fixed (usually on a 50:50 basis, but it can be in any proportion) and separate, so that each person can separately dispose of his or her share by will. If you don't state the shares the law assumes a 50:50 split.

Problems with solicitors

Do you have a remedy against the solicitors who helped you buy the home?

If you bought the home jointly, or transferred it into your joint names you ought to have been given sensible advice by the solicitors who dealt with the purchase so you knew the implications of what you were doing. The Court of Appeal (in Springette -v-Defoe see below) said that it is probably negligent if the solicitor does not find out and record at the time of the conveyance what the joint purchasers' shares of the property are agreed to be.

If your solicitor failed to do this and you end up having to pay for legal costs to establish your rights in the home, or you end up with a court case where you end up losing part of the property, you may be able to recoup some of your loss from your original solicitor. You can explore the possibilities with your current solicitor - unless of course you are still using the same one. If this is the case then you will need to take advice from another firm.

there may be reasons why this is not fair. The situation may have changed; one of you may have contributed far more than the other, one of you may have misled the other. If you cannot renegotiate a split that you feel is fair you may have to ask a judge to decide. In a court hearing the judge will have to decide whose evidence he or she finds the most convincing.

Case Study Miss Springette

Common Intention: A Case Study

Miss Springette and Mr Defoe lived together for three years before deciding to buy a house, raising the mortgage together. Miss Springette contributed about 75 per cent of the purchase price as she provided almost all of the deposit and she was entitled to the Council discount under the 'right to buy' scheme. However, when they bought the house it was put into their joint names, effectively giving it to them in equal shares. There was no declaration about the contribution that each had made.

When the relationship broke up about three years after the purchase, Mr Defoe went to court to try to get half of the house. The judge who first heard the case took the view that they were entitled to equal shares, despite the unequal contributions, because this must have been their 'common intention'.

Luckily for Miss Springette, the Court of Appeal took a different view and said that there could not have a 'common intention' as this could not have been communicated to each other. One judge said, 'Our trust law does not allow property rights to be affected by telepathy.' As there was no evidence that the couple had discussed that they would share the property equally, their entitlement was based upon the shares in which they had contributed.

The crucial point to note in this case is that there was evidence that the couple had never discussed how they were going to hold the property. In most relationships it will be hard to establish a negative like this; if you have talked about buying a home together, you are likely to have discussed how you will own it. It is always better to be explicit, and if possible record your intentions in writing.

When a court can alter an agreement

There are two sets of circumstances in which, despite an original agreement, you may end up having a legal dispute:

- The first is where the dispute concerns the terms of the original agreement. In these cases, the court will have to investigate the facts. In the absence of any other argument, on either side, the court would declare your shares in the home to be as it finds they were originally arranged.

- The second is where one or both of you argues that there is a very good reason for the court to judge that you can depart from the original agreement. This is likely to be for one of two main reasons. The first is where you have subsequently renegotiated the agreement. You may have formally recorded this or you may have simply relied on what you saw as a mutual understanding that the situation had changed. Here, again, the court would be concerned to establish what really happened between you, and divide the home accordingly. The second is where events or actions after the original agreement have been so inconsistent with the original agreement that the logical conclusion is that there

must have been a variation or cancellation of the agreement. An example of this would be where you agreed to hold the house in equal shares on the understanding that you would both contribute equally to the purchase price and the mortgage; subsequently one of you has paid little or nothing. Here, the court would not only look at what had actually happened but also at what would be fair or appropriate, given the original intention of the agreement.

The court can look at all the circumstances during your relationship, but one of the key factors will be the contribution that you have each made in money, or in kind, to the purchase or improvement of the home. Payments of money can be 'treated as illuminating the common intention as to the extent of the beneficial interest'.

THE HOME IN ONE PERSON'S NAME

Where the home is in the name of one of you only, there is a different set of legal remedies and considerations. The straightforward common law position says that the non-owner has no interest in the home, but English law also has a set of what are called 'equitable principles'. These can override the common law to make sure that a fairer result is achieved. But you have still to ensure that your case comes within the established criteria laid down as precedents by a whole line of cases.

TRUSTS

The court can look at your relationship to decide whether it can find evidence that a 'trust' has been created. A trust in this context would mean that the ownership of the property should be shared in some way.

The court can decide that there has been an 'express trust', which is nothing to do with its speed, but that it has been expressed or declared in some way - you could have done this in a living together agreement.

Implied trust

If there has not been an express trust there may be an implied trust. The court can take the view that there must, or ought to have been a trust of the home because of the way that you have both behaved. For instance, if you have both contributed to the payment when the house was bought, or to the mortgage repayments. Contributions can include financial contributions to the whole running of the household, not just direct payments to the purchase of the house. Also you may be able either to claim a share of the sale proceeds or prevent the home being sold over your head if you can rely on something called 'proprietary

estoppel'. To be able to rely on this you must show that the owner has behaved in such a way that you were led to believe that you would have a right in the home, whether to a share or to a right to occupy it. And, based on this belief, you have acted to your detriment. You might have done this by making financial contributions to the home or by doing improvements to it. You need not always have made yourself financially worse off; you might, for instance, have given up your home and come to live with your partner, relying on his or her promises that you would have a home with him or her for life.

Was there an understanding or agreement?

You will need to establish what your original understanding or agreement was. This may not be disputed, but as you are both going to want a version of events which best serves your own purposes, there is likely to be an argument over the original facts. Unless you can agree, broadly speaking, on what was originally said, or implied, the court will have to make a finding about which version the judge thinks is the more probable.

Has the non owner acted to his or her detriment?

You then have to show what the non owner has done in reliance on the promises. You might have paid towards the purchase of the home either directly, by contributing towards the purchase price, or the mortgage. Or you might have made indirect payments, paying for something else and freeing the owner's money to be used for the purchase. You might have helped with the cost of decorating or maintaining the home, or you might have helped in kind, with repairs or renovations.

You might have made no actual contribution in this way but still lost out as a result of your reliance on the owner. You might have given up your home and job in order to live together.

What the court can do

The court can decide whether you ought to have a share in the home, (and how big that share ought to be) or whether you have the right to live in the home for a fixed period, or for life.

IN A HOME THAT YOU RENT

The legal position regarding rented accommodation depends on the sort of tenancy that you have (see Appendix). The following is only a very brief guide and you will need to take specialist advice about your position. See *The Which? Essential Guide Renting and Letting* for more information. In most cases the court does have power to transfer a tenancy between cohabitants, if the tenancy has not been terminated by a notice to quit.

Jargon buster

Types of tenancies. Your tenancy agreement may state what sort of tenancy you have. If it is not clear look at the explanations below:

Assured shorthold tenancy and assured tenancy: If it started on or after 28th February 1997 unless the landlord has stated in writing that it is an assured tenancy. If it started from 15th January 1989 to and 27th February 1997 it will be an assured shorthold tenancy if the landlord stated it to be so on a legal form when it first started. If he did not, then it is an assured tenancy. Housing Association tenancies from 15th January 1989 generally come into this category.

Regulated or protected tenancy: If your tenancy started before 15th January 1989 it will generally be a regulated or protected tenancy.

Secure tenancy: Most Council tenancies unless they are in temporary accommodation. Housing Association tenancies that started before 15th January 1989.

Periodic tenancy: Periodic tenancies have no fixed end date when you sign the original agreement and simply continue from week to week, or month to month (depending on how you pay your rent) until either you or the landlord gives the appropriate notice.

Fixed term tenancy: A tenancy for a limited period – six months is typical

Statutory periodic tenancy: A tenancy that continues after the fixed term ends.

Sorting out your shares when you own the family home

Is the home in joint names or one person's name?

Sole

Joint

Non-owner can make a claim if he/she can show that a trust has been created, explicitly or implicitly:
• Owner has promised a share in return for a contribution.
• Owner has made promises which have made the non-owner act to his/her detriment.

Is it a tenancy in common or a joint tenancy? (see j b box on page...).

TIC

JT

You are entitled to the home in the shares in the original deed. If none stated, 50% each.

You are You are entitled to 50% each

However, there are factors that might alter the legal shares, such as:
• An agreement between you.•
• A change in circumstances that changes the original understanding.

Your interests in other property

There are no legal proceedings designed to allow cohabitants to make claims against each other to sort out ownership of possessions. This means the court treats you as any two people who have a dispute over ownership.

The fact that you have had a family relationship is all but irrelevant. The only exception to this is if you are a male-female couple and have been engaged. This brings you within the scope of the Married Women's Property Act 1882, and the court can say who owns disputed items of property (including your home) if you apply within three years of the termination of the engagement.

If you did not have an agreement about the things that you bought together and need to sort them out now, try to do it together. You can make a list of all the items and then try to sort out who should have what. You can decide how you want to do this. You may want to divide on the basis of the price that you paid for them, you may want to look at their value now, rather than at the date of purchase. You may want to achieve a rough equality in the sorts of things that you have, so that one has the sitting room suite, and one the dining table and chairs, for instance. You can decide that the fairest way is to take it in turns to choose, or discuss items room by room. It really does not matter how you do it, provided you find a way of reaching an agreement. If you cannot do this without the help of someone else, this is a good thing to take to a mediation service.

In most cases, you will not be able to establish ownership by referring to documents. A car may be registered in a person's name, but

> **! Health warning!**
> You need to think carefully about starting a legal claim. Few domestic assets have such value that you can justify the amount that you will spend in legal costs sorting out a dispute over them. You will probably spend far more on lawyers than the value of the item.

Rules about ownership: The legal position outlined

- If you bought something, and you alone paid for it, it belongs to you.
- If you bought something out of joint funds, without distinguishing in what shares you contributed, you own it jointly and equally.
- If you bought something and contributed unequally, then you own it in the shares in which you contributed to its purchase.
- If one of you gave the other something, it belongs to the person it was given to. This includes engagement rings, even if you never marry.

Try to list your personal items together so that you can work out the best way to divide them.

that is not conclusive proof of ownership; in the absence of a gift or a promise, the car would belong to the person who paid for it.

These rules can be upset by what you do or say to each other. If you buy something with your money but say to your partner, 'this belongs to both of us', or, 'this is yours' and behave as though you mean it, then a court can hold you to your promise. You can be regarded as having created 'a trust' of the property. You might do this consciously - as you do if you enter into a living together agreement. Or a court can find that you have created a trust by implication; your behaviour or what you have said lead to the conclusion that the

property should, for reasons of fairness, be shared or even transferred to your partner.

There does have to be a shared, or communicated, intention to share the property however.

BANK AND OTHER ACCOUNTS

On the face of it, if you have a joint account with your partner, you hold it in equal shares and things that you buy from it are owned jointly and equally. But this is not always the case. If only one of you puts money into the account though you can both draw on it, the strict legal construction would be that money and any purchases made from it would belong to the person putting the money in. The strict legal position can be over-ridden by an agreement between you, or by your behaviour giving rise to a trust as described above.

PREVIOUSLY-OWNED POSSESSIONS

These will be your own individual property unless you have made gifts of them to each other. There could also be circumstances in which you have started to treat such items as belonging to you both and you have both contributed to their maintenance. For example, if you helped to restore and maintain a classic car that was owned by your partner prior to the relationship. You may have contributed financially, as well as giving up your time. When you split up you could justify a claim to a share of the car on the basis that you had been led to believe that you had an interest in it and had acted to your detriment in helping restore it.

WHAT IF YOU ARE STILL PAYING FOR THINGS WHEN YOU SPLIT UP?

If you have bought things using a credit card, H.P. agreement or loan the person who made the credit agreement is liable for the repayments, as far as the lender is concerned. And you are jointly and severally liable if you took the loan out together.

The logical position ought to be that if you are paying for something, you ought to have it, unless you have said to your partner that you are buying the thing for him or her, and in effect, already made a gift of it. If you were buying something jointly you will have to decide between you who is going to go on making the payments and who will have the object. The credit company will not be bound by your decision that only one of you is going to be responsible for the payments, but it would be worth

Jargon buster

Jointly and severally liable: Either of you can be sued for the whole of the debt.

explaining to them the arrangement that you have made in any event, and telling them your new address(es). The reason for this is that if your partner says that he or she will take on the repayments and does not make them, the company can take debt recovery proceedings, and will name both of you. You do not have to be personally served with the proceedings; they can post them to your last address. You might find that a judgment had been obtained against you without your having had the chance to defend the proceedings. Judgments like this can affect your credit rating.

Applying to the court for an order

As there is no umbrella legislation to protect cohabitants, you have to use a number of ways to bring claims to court.

This book can only give you a very brief outline of the procedure in each case. You will need to take specialist legal advice if you intend to proceed with a claim. We would strongly advise you to consider using mediation to reach a settlement (see Chapter 4).

Applying for a share in an owned home

Relevant law	Trusts of Land and Appointment of Trustees Act 1996, section 14
What the court must consider	• The intentions of the person or persons who created the trust • The purposes for which the home subject to the trust is held • The welfare of any child who occupies or might reasonably be expected the home • The interests of any secured creditor of any beneficiary
What the court can do	• Declare who owns the home and in what shares. • Order a sale of the property • Order one person to pay the other a sum of money in return for their assessed share
How do you apply	On form N1 or N208 (Part 8 claim form) with evidence set out in a sworn statement. You have to serve any mortgagee as well as the owner. County Court Fee: £150 (Exemption form EX160)

If you want the home for you and any children, you can combine this claim with one for them under the Children Act 1989. If you don't succeed on your own account, you might be able to keep a home for the children.

 Courts service: www.hmcourts-service.gov.uk Leaflet 208a.

Applying for a transfer of property order for the children

Relevant law	**Children Act 1989, Schedule 1**

What the court must consider	• Your income, earning capacity, property and other financial resources, now and in the future.
	• Your needs, obligations and responsibilities.
	• The children's needs.
	• Any income or other financial resources that belong to the children.
	• Any physical or mental disability of any child.
	• The way in which the child was being brought up and educated.
	• If the order is against a person who is not the child's parent, the court must also consider:
	  o To what extent that person has assumed responsibility for the child.
	  o Whether he or she knew that he/she was not the child's parent.
	  o Whether there is anyone else who is liable to support the child.

What the court can do	As well as maintenance and lump sum payments the court can order a transfer of property order, either to the person who applies for the order for the benefit of the child, or to the child him or herself.
How do you apply	On Form C1 and C10 in the County Court with a statement of means form on C10A. Fee: £175 (county court). (Exemption form EX160.)

Under a Children Act application the court will generally not transfer a home to a parent outright. Instead, you might get the right to live in the home while the children are still in full time education. You should consider combining an application under this Act with one for yourself for a transfer of tenancy or a declaration of your interest in the home.

Courts Service : www.hmcourts-service.gov.uk
Leaflet CB1.

Applying for a transfer of a tenancy

Relevant law	Part IV of the Family Law Act 1996, Schedule 7

What the court must consider	• The circumstances in which the tenancy was originally granted.
	• Each person's housing needs and those of any child living with you.
	• Your financial resources.
	• The likely effect if the court orders, or does not order, on the health, safety and wellbeing of each of you and of any child.
	• If only one of you is the tenant:
	  o the nature of your relationship.
	  o the length of time you have lived together.
	  o whether you have any children.
	  o how long it is since you separated.

What the court can do	• Transfer a tenancy between you. • Order (if appropriate) the person who gets the tenancy to pay the other a lump sum. • Order who is liable for any unpaid debts.
How do you apply	On Form M23 in the county court. Landlord must also be served. County Court Fee: £60. (Exemption form EX160.)

COSTS

The rules about how costs are awarded are not the same as the rules for proceedings in the context of divorce. The various procedures described in this Chapter are more adversarial. Costs can be awarded against the 'loser' in the case. You and your solicitor will have to think carefully about the way you negotiate and the offers that you make to settle the case. If you receive proposals for settlement you must consider them carefully. If you refuse to settle and the case goes to court you will need to get a better order than the offer or risk being liable for costs.

When you get a court order

See Chapter 9 page 195 onwards about what to do with your order and enforcement.

Ownership of property if you have been engaged

This only applies to male-female couples. The Civil Partnership Act has not amended the law to include a couple engaging to enter into a civil partnership. This may be open to a challenge but there is, as yet, no established law on the point. 'Property' includes ownership of a home, so if you have been engaged it may be helpful to combine this with a TOLATA application. You must apply within three years of the termination of the engagement.

Relevant law	**Married Women's Property Act 1882, section 17.**
What the court must consider	Principles of ownership as they exist in common law – established rules and case law.
What the court can do	• Say who is entitled to property and in what shares. • Order property to be sold. • Order payment of a lump sum. •Prevent disposal of an asset.
How do you apply	In form M23 in the county court with a supporting sworn statement. Fee: £ 200. (Exemption Form EX160.)

Application to sort out ownership of disputed property

Relevant law	**Common Law**
What the court must consider	Principles of ownership as they exist in common law – established rules and case law.
What the court can do	• Say who is entitled to property and in what shares. • Prevent disposal of an asset
How do you apply	In the Small Claims Court if the item is under £5,000, otherwise in the County Court. The fee depends on the item or amount. £150 if it is property as opposed to money. (Exemption Form EX160.)

 Courts Service www.hmcourts-service.gov.uk
Leaflets on how to bring a claim EX301 and EX 302.

Other Parts of the UK

This chapter highlights the differences in the law in Scotland and Northern Ireland, each of which is a separate legal jurisdiction from England and Wales.

PART 4

11

Scotland

For your convenience, this has been arranged to highlight the difference chapter by chapter in the rest of the book. The Civil Partnership Act 2004 is in force in both Scotland and Northern Ireland. As in England and Wales it mirrors matrimonial law in both jurisdictions.

CHAPTER 1 LEGAL COSTS

If there is no agreement as to divorce expenses, the court will apportion them at the end of the proceedings. The main factors that influence the courts are which spouse won and whether each spouse conducted the proceedings in a responsible way. For example, if you make exaggerated claims or are uncooperative, thus forcing your spouse/cp to litigate unnecessarily, you could end up paying most of your spouse/cp's expenses as well as your own. Often no award is made, so each spouse/cp is left to pay his or her own expenses. The courts are reluctant to order a

 The Family Law (Scotland) Act 2006 which came into force on 4th May 2006, has brought a number of changes to Scottish family law including 'DIY divorces'.

legally aided spouse/cp to pay the other's expenses.

It is common for consent to be given to a one years' non-cohabitation divorce on condition that the consenting spouse will not be liable for the other's expenses.

For proceedings other than divorce proceedings, the normal rule is that the loser pays the winner's expenses as well as his or her own.

Even if your spouse pays your expenses you will almost certainly be out of pocket, as the court's award is unlikely to meet the costs of the litigation, let alone all consultations with your solicitor and other extras which your spouse is not required to pay for.

Legal aid

Legal aid is available for court proceedings: divorce, financial claims and matters concerning the children or housing, whether with the divorce

 Scottish Legal Aid Board: 0131 226 7061 www.slab.org.uk

proceedings or separately. Your solicitor will help you apply for legal advice and assistance, or legal aid. The Scottish Legal Aid Board runs both schemes.

The Scottish Legal Aid Board deducts the amount of your expenses from money the court awards you, or property that the court orders to be transferred to you, if it cannot recover the sum in full from your contributions or from your opponent. However, no deduction is made from any aliment (money paid periodically for a person's support) or periodical allowance or the first £4,653 of any capital sum or transfer of property awarded (as from 6 April 2006).

CHAPTER 2 FINANCIAL PLANNING

The Matrimonial Homes (Family Protection) (Scotland) Act 1981 gives you certain rights if you do not own the home and your spouse is the sole owner. You are entitled to continue to occupy and live in the home. Moreover, your consent is required for any sale or other disposal, although the court can dispense with your consent if it is being withheld unreasonably. These rights are automatic: you do not have to register them in the Land

 Married co-tenants and spouses/ CPs of sole tenants have similar protection against the tenancy of the home being given up.

Register for Scotland or the Register of Sasines (public registers of property and its owners).

You can renounce your occupancy rights, but it is seldom in your interest to do so. A renunciation must be in writing and signed and declared before a notary public.

CHAPTER 3 GETTING LEGAL ADVICE

The Family Law Association in Scotland has a comprehensive list of solicitors who practice in family law. The Law Society of Scotland have a list of solicitors who are accredited as specialists in Family Law. Alternatively, your library or CAB should have lists showing which local solicitors undertake divorce work and whether they will act for clients on legal aid. The Law Society of Scotland will also help you find a solicitor.

CHAPTER 5 DIVORCE AND CHILDREN

The Children Act 1989 does not apply to Scotland; the legislation applicable is the Children (Scotland) Act 1995. In Scotland parents have various legal responsibilities towards their children, such as safeguarding them, advising them and acting on their behalf in legal transactions; and various rights, such as deciding where they are to live, controlling their upbringing and having contact with them.

These responsibilities and rights cease when the children reach 16. The children can then live where they like, look after their own money and generally make their own decisions. A child under 16 can consent to medical treatment if the doctor thinks that he or she can understand what the proposed treatment involves, and in such a case the parents cannot overrule the child.

While parents live together they share parental responsibilities and rights. Each can act alone, neither can veto the other's actions, and any irreconcilable disputes have to be resolved by the courts. On divorce the court may, on application, reallocate these responsibilities and rights. Orders may be unnecessary if the parents are going to cooperate or if the non-resident parent will not interfere with the day-to-day decisions of the parent looking after the children. Otherwise the parent who is going to be looking after the children may need to apply for a residence order, which will give him or her the right to have the children living with him or her in addition to the other responsibilities and rights. The other parent retains these except in relation to the children's residence.

If the parents cannot agree which of them the children should live with, the court will decide on welfare grounds, taking any views

expressed by the children into account. Children of 12 and over are presumed able to form a view, and courts rarely go against firm views of 14- or 15-year-olds. Children below 12 can also give the court their views, which will be taken into account, but they may not be regarded as conclusive.

CHAPTER 6 CHILD MAINTENANCE

The CSA now assesses maintenance for children up to and including 18 years of age who are still in secondary education. Currently the courts have no power to deal with claims for aliment made for these children. Certain categories of children as described in Chapter 6 are not within the Agency's remit and can still be awarded aliment by the courts. Children have to look after themselves once they reach 25, as the parental obligation of aliment ceases then. A formal registered agreement for child maintenance (aliment) has the same effect as a court order in England, and excludes the CSA jurisdiction unless the recipient goes onto benefit. The amount of aliment a court can award depends on what the person paying it can afford and what the child needs. The previous level of support the child enjoyed is also important. A child over 11 can apply to the CSA for an assessment of his or her own maintenance. Children over 18 who wish aliment via the courts must claim themselves. Below that age a parent may claim on their behalf.

CHAPTER 7 EMERGENCIES

You can be protected from harm by obtaining an 'interdict', which you may need to combine with an exclusion order (see boxes below).

An interdict orders the Defender not to assault, threaten or harass the Pursuer. It can also be used to protect children. It can restrain the Defender from coming near your home.

If you need to exclude your partner from the home you will need to apply for an exclusion order as well.

Interdicts

Married couples/CPS 'matrimonial interdicts'	Cohabiting couples 'domestic interdicts'
"child" is a "child of the family" and includes any child or grandchild of either spouse – and any person who has been brought up or treated by either spouse as if they were a child of that spouse, whatever the age.	"child" is any child in the permanent or temporary care of the Pursuer, and is thus restricted to children under 16 years.

Exclusion orders

Married couples/CPs	Cohabiting couples
You have rights of occupancy whether or not you are the owner or tenant of the home.	You do not have automatic occupancy rights unless you are the sole or joint owner/tenant of the home.
Your spouse/cp cannot legally exclude you from the house, and the police will help you get back in if you are evicted.	You can apply for occupancy rights at the same time as you ask for an exclusion order.
You can apply for an exclusion order which generally lasts until the marriage ends on divorce. You can apply for this order as part of the divorce proceedings.	If you are the sole owner/tenancy, you do not need to apply for an order unless your partner has already been granted occupancy rights: you can simply tell them to leave. If they don't you can get a summary ejection order.

If the court is satisfied, first, that the (interim) exclusion order is necessary to protect you and/or the children it then has to consider whether it is reasonable for him or her to be excluded. Your spouse must be sent a copy of your application for an (interim) exclusion order and given an opportunity to oppose it. You will have to back up your claim with as much evidence as you can, such as affidavits from your doctor or neighbours about your health and past incidents of violence, reports by the police if they have been involved, and evidence of your need for the home and the unsuitable nature of your present temporary accommodation if you have been forced to leave home.

The Protection from Harassment Act

This 1997 Act (Sections 8 to 11) applies to Scotland. There is no necessity for there to be any defined relationship between Pursuer and Defender. For example, this could be used after a divorce. A person must not pursue a 'course of conduct' which amounts to harassment. There must be at least two occasions on which the conduct has taken place. There is no provision for interim Non-Harassment Orders, and therefore interdict and interim interdict are often sought in the same action, if immediate protection is required.

However, the Defender cannot be subject to the same prohibitions in an interdict and a Non-Harassment order in the same action. Breach of a Non-Harassment Order is a criminal offence.

Powers of Arrest

A power of arrest can be attached to an interdict where protection from abuse was sought. Once the power of arrest is granted you must inform both the defender and the Chief Constable of the local Police Force. A constable can then arrest the defender without warrant if he has reasonable cause for suspecting that there has been a breach of interdict and that he considers that. if the person was not arrested, there would be a risk of abuse or further abuse. Criminal proceedings may be brought. If not, the Sheriff, after enquiry, can still order the Defender's further detention for up to two more days.

Child abduction

The Scottish provisions of the Child Abduction Act 1984 are different from those for England and Wales. A parent commits a criminal offence by taking a child out of the UK only if:

- the other parent (or someone else) has a residence order (or in old cases, was awarded custody) and has not agreed to the child's removal, or
- the court has interdicted removal.

If your spouse is likely to take the children abroad, you should at once apply for a residence order or an interdict. You can do so even without applying for divorce, but if you have started divorce proceedings the application has to be made in the context of those proceedings. In an emergency you can obtain an interdict at any hour of the day or night. Once you have an interdict or a residence order, you can ask the police and sheriff officers to trace the children and prevent their removal from the country. You should also ask the police for a Port-Stop Order.

CHAPTER 8 GETTING A DIVORCE / DISSOLUTION

Jurisdiction: One or both of you needs to be habitually resident or domiciled in Scotland.

Judicial separation

The court granting a judicial separation has no power to award a capital sum or order a transfer of property: it can only award aliment for you. You and your spouse remain married to each other, so neither of you can remarry. There is limited legal point in getting a judicial separation, because now you can get aliment from the court without asking for separation, but a few couples still opt for a judicial separation for religious reasons.

A husband does not inherit any of the property the wife acquired after judicial separation if she dies without having made a will. There is no equivalent rule disinheriting a separated wife.

There is no minimum period you have to wait after marriage before you can bring divorce proceedings.

Grounds for divorce

There are only four facts on which you can base a petition for divorce to show that the marriage has irretrievably broken down. CPs have only three facts, as adultery is not available to them. You can also have a divorce on the basis that an interim gender recognition certificate has been issued to one of the parties after the marriage.

The facts on which you can base a petition for divorce

1: adultery
2: unreasonable behaviour
3: non-cohabitation for a period of one or more years with consent of the other person
4: non-cohabitation for a period of two years.

 DIY court forms are available from the courts or Citizens Advice Bureaux (CABx). Or go to www.scotcourts.gov.uk to download them. Help leaflets are also available.

Which court?

Most divorces are dealt with in the sheriff courts. These are local courts situated in most major towns in Scotland. You can bring proceedings in the court for the area in which you or your spouse/cp have been living for the past 40 days; you would usually choose your own local court. Divorces are also heard in the Court of Session in Edinburgh. Divorces are usually heard in the Court of Session if the case is more complex, difficult or large sums of money are involved.

There are no decrees nisi or absolute in Scotland. The court grants a single decree of divorce which is immediately effective, although a certain period (14 days in the sheriff court, 21 days in the Court of Session) is allowed for an appeal.

Getting a divorce

There are two types of procedure: the simplified procedure (usually called a DIY divorce), and the ordinary procedure.

Ordinary procedure

This is more complex and you are strongly advised to get a solicitor to act for you. Most divorces are heard in the sheriff courts, so only that procedure will be described here.

 You do not need a solicitor for a DIY divorce. However, it is a good idea to get legal advice before you start in order to make sure that you are fully aware of the consequences and that you are not losing rights in ignorance.

Fees for swearing an affidavit

Before a notary public - most solicitors - (for a fee)

Before a justice of the peace (free)

The Court of Session procedure is slightly different. Proceedings start

DIY Procedure

One year + non-cohab with consent

Complete part 1 of form. Spouse/cp completes part 2 of form. You swear affadavit on part 3 of form.

Send completed form to court with:
- Marriage certificate
- Court due £62 (exempt if you are on legal aid).

Court tells you when divorce is granted, usually about 2 months.

Two years + non-cohab with consent

Complete part 1 of form. You swear affadavit on part 3 of form.

with your solicitor lodging the initial writ in court. This document sets out briefly the facts of your case and details the orders you are asking the court to make. A copy of this writ is then served on your spouse/cp. You are called the pursuer and he or she is the defender. A copy also has to be served on any person (a co-defender) with whom you aver your spouse has committed adultery. The children may be sent a notice telling them about the court proceedings (if a parental rights order is sought), unless the court considers it inappropriate because of the children's age, and they will be invited to express their views either in person or in writing. In a divorce action based on either one or two years' non-cohabitation, your spouse is also sent a notice warning of the possible financial

DIY divorces – only on the fact of non-cohabitation facts 3 & 4

Conditions:
- no children of the marriage under 16 years of age
- no financial claims by you or your spouse/cp
- no other legal proceedings affecting your marriage waiting to be heard
- the divorce is not defended
- neither you nor your spouse/cp must be suffering from a mental disorder

consequences of divorce (loss of pension or inheritance rights, for example). The notice alerts your spouse to the financial and other applications he or she can make to the court.

In your initial writ you can apply for various interim orders, or you can add them on later (which will incur extra court fees). Interim orders last until the divorce is granted, when the position is reviewed and fresh orders made. Examples of interim orders are:

- interim aliment for you. The CSA deals with maintenance for the children, unless the parent against whom the order is sought is out of the UK
- interim residence for and contact with the children
- an interim interdict (order) against violent behaviour or disposal of assets
- an interdict against taking the children out of Scotland. Your application for this need not be intimated to your spouse/cp, so that he or she may get no warning at all
- an exclusion order excluding your spouse/cp from the family home.

You can also apply for these remedies separately; they are available not only in divorce proceedings. If you cannot apply for a divorce as soon as you and your spouse/cp split up, you may need to use separate proceedings.

Defences

A notice of intention to defend must be lodged within 21 days (42 if the defender is abroad). The court will then specify the date defences have to be lodged by and the date of the options hearing (see below). In your defences you can oppose your spouse/cp's claims and/or make claims against him or her. Each of you will then adjust your case to meet the other's. An options hearing will then be held during which the court will clarify the issues in dispute and decide how to proceed. You and your spouse/cp and your respective solicitors are required to attend, but you or your spouse may be excused. Some courts involve the couple in the discussions, others listen only to the solicitors.

It is unusual for the divorce itself to be defended. More commonly your spouse/cp will defend your application for financial orders or matters relating to the children, or will apply for similar orders. Where the divorce is defended, the case is heard in court with each side and their witnesses giving evidence. Where only financial aspects are at issue, the divorce itself can be disposed of on the basis of sworn statements (affidavits) containing full information about your and your spouse/cp's financial resources (income and capital) and needs. Oral evidence is still required for all the issues that remain in dispute.

Affidavits

An affidavit is accepted by the court as evidence of the facts contained in it. You, your spouse/cp and others can give evidence by affidavits instead of attending court, but this is not advisable unless the action is undefended or the evidence is uncontroversial. Your solicitor will prepare your affidavit from the information you give, and you will then swear it before¶ation must be up to date, complete and accurate; otherwise further affidavits or oral evidence will be called for. Deliberately concealing facts, or making false statements, is regarded as a very serious offence for which you could well be imprisoned.

The children

You should show that satisfactory arrangements have been made for any children of the marriage who are under 16. Most couples reach agreement about who is to look after the children. You or your spouse/cp's affidavit will state who is going to look after the children, how they are going to be looked after, and what accommodation will be available for them. In addition, the court requires an affidavit from a relative or a person (such as a neighbour) who knows the children well. If these affidavits are satisfactory, the court will accept the arrangements without interviewing the couple or the children.

If you or your spouse/cp apply for an order in relation to the children, a child welfare hearing will be fixed. This hearing takes place on the first convenient date three weeks after lodging the notice of intention to defend. You will both be expected to attend; the children may attend and may be given an opportunity to make their views known. The court may decide the matter there and then, it may refer you both to mediation or it may postpone the matter to a later date for more thorough consideration. If the outcome is the last of these, the court may ask an independent person to prepare a report. The reporter is often an advocate or solicitor, but sometimes a social worker is used. The court will consider this report along with all the evidence from witnesses and other sources before deciding what would be best for the children's welfare.

Joint minute

If you and your spouse/cp can agree on the financial aspects and future arrangements for the children before proceedings start, you can ask the court simply to make the appropriate orders and your spouse/cp need not defend. An alternative, which is sometimes adopted, is for a formal enforceable agreement to be prepared covering these matters (this is similar to a separation agreement). In these circumstances, you can then apply to the court for divorce – divorce being the only order sought. In some cases a DIY divorce may be possible. In many cases, however, agreement is reached only after proceedings have started, as a result of negotiation or mediation. You and your spouse/cp will then arrange for your respective solicitors to submit a joint minute to the court. This minute either sets out the orders that you and your spouse/cp request the court to grant, or asks the court to make no orders because the matters are to be covered by a written agreement. The terms of the joint minute should be checked carefully. Once it has been lodged in court it is normally impossible to change your mind and ask the court to do something else.

Where the proceedings are undefended or a joint minute is submitted, the court will normally grant the orders sought without further enquiry. The court may, however, demand further information in matters affecting the children.

Decree

A decree is a formal document containing the orders made by the court. The financial orders are almost always granted at the same time as the divorce, although it is possible, in certain circumstances, to have these left over for a later hearing.

The court will notify you that decree has been granted and also notify your spouse/cp if his or her address is known. There is a 14-day period allowed for appeal (21 days in the Court of Session). After that, an extract (certified copy) of the decree, which details the orders the court made, can be obtained from the court. You will need an extract to show that you are divorced if you plan to marry again, and also to enforce the orders if your spouse/cp refuses to pay.

CHAPTER 9 MONEY IN DIVORCE

The court on granting divorce may:
- make no order and allow the home to be sold; the proceeds will have been taken into account in any lump-sum award made
- transfer the ownership (or tenancy) of the home or a share of it from one of you to the other. The date of transfer can be deferred, but delays of more than a few months to allow time for the legal documents to be prepared are not common
- regulate who is to occupy the home after divorce. This is not often done, but it might be used for instance to allow a wife and children to continue to occupy the home owned by her husband until she can get a job and afford somewhere else. An express exclusion of her husband from the home might be necessary if he was likely to interfere with her occupation of the home.

Financial orders

The main financial orders the court can make on divorce are:
- ordering one spouse to pay a lump sum (a 'capital' sum) to the other; and/or
- ordering one spouse to pay the other a periodical allowance – a regular sum each week or month; and/or
- ordering a spouse to pay aliment for the children of the marriage, but only if the CSA cannot assess maintenance; and/or
- transferring the ownership of property from one spouse to the other.
- Ordering a spouse to split their pension with the other.

It is possible, but unusual, for the court to grant a divorce and postpone the financial orders to a later date if disagreement is holding up the divorce.

The court can also order the house to be sold immediately or at a later date and/or say who is to occupy it and to have use of the contents. Where the house is rented, the court can transfer the tenancy from one spouse to the other.

Either the pursuer or the defender can apply for financial orders. You have to state in your initial writ or defences exactly what orders you seek from the court and give evidence of your and your spouse's needs and resources to demonstrate that they are reasonable claims. The court also needs to know the amount of aliment currently being paid. Making exaggerated claims is a bad tactic, as it will merely get your spouse's back up and possibly have a bearing on any sympathy the Court may have with you or your spouse. This may result in your having to pay your spouse's legal costs. Almost inevitably a couple's living standards drop after divorce. A fair settlement should result in this drop being shared between the spouses.

A claim for a lump sum or transfer of property must be made before the divorce is granted. You can claim periodical allowance afterwards but you are very unlikely to get it then, because the principles required to justify an award (principles 3 to 5 below), generally speaking, apply to your situation at the time of divorce. You cannot claim periodical allowance later if at the time of divorce you and your spouse made a formal agreement that you would not claim.

The Family Law (Scotland) Act 1985 sets out a series of principles to guide the court in making financial orders, as follows.

1.Sharing matrimonial property.
This includes:
- the home and its contents, savings, investments and other assets which you or your spouse/cp own and which were acquired between the date of marriage and the date of final separation.
- The home and contents are also counted as matrimonial assets if they were acquired before marriage as a family home for the couple, even if the house is in the name of one spouse/cp only.
- Lump sum payable on retirement and pensions.

 Assets given to you or inherited by you are not regarded as matrimonial property.

Matrimonial property should be shared equally unless there is a good reason for unequal division, which might be ordered where, say, your parents helped you buy the home or where you run a business that cannot be divided.

2. Balancing economic advantages and disadvantages
The court has to take account of your financial and non-financial contributions to your spouse/cp's wealth – and the other way round. Examples include helping with the running costs of the home, sacrificing a career to look after the children or working in your spouse/cp's business at an artificially low wage.

3. Sharing childcare

Future childcare costs are to be shared. These include your loss of earnings while looking after the children and the expense of keeping up a larger and more expensive house than you would need if you were living on your own. If maintenance for the children is assessed by the CSA, it includes an amount for childcare costs; the court will then take account of this principle only for extra costs.

4. Financial dependency

Under this principle you are entitled to support for up to three years after divorce, to enable you to become self-supporting if you were financially dependent upon your spouse/cp during the marriage.

5. Severe financial hardship

If you are unlikely to be self-supporting after divorce (too old or ill, for example), you may need support for many years (the rest of your life, perhaps) to avoid severe financial hardship.

Court orders

Principles 1 and 2 can be satisfied only by the award of a lump sum and/or a transfer of property. The lump sum may be payable all at once, shortly after divorce or at a specified later date, or by instalments. Principles 3 to 5 should be satisfied by a lump sum or transfer of property if possible, otherwise by a periodical allowance. If you are looking after young children you may be able to get a periodical allowance under principle 3 as compensation for loss of earnings or the childcare costs if you work.

If a periodical allowance at the time of divorce cannot be justified by principles 3, 4 or 5, a spouse/cp will not be awarded one. The court will not award a nominal periodical allowance on divorce with the intention that it could be increased later if the recipient's financial circumstances get worse.

Change in circumstances

After divorce your or your ex-spouse/cp's financial circumstances may change. You may be able to go back to court to get your orders changed, depending on the type of order involved.

Lump-sum order

You cannot apply for a lump-sum order after divorce. If you were awarded a lump sum on divorce the court cannot generally change the amount payable. The only exception is a rare one. If the true facts were concealed from the court or lies were told to obtain the original order, the court can make a new order. Apart from this exceptional case, all the court can do is to alter the way in which the lump sum is paid, perhaps by ordering payment by instalments or giving more time to pay.

Property-transfer orders

You cannot apply for a transfer of property order after divorce. If you were awarded a transfer on divorce, the court cannot alter the property to be transferred except in the circumstances mentioned above. All it can do is to alter the date set for transfer.

Periodical allowance

You can apply for a periodical allowance after divorce, but it would be awarded only in unusual circumstances. You cannot apply if you agreed not to do so as part of the divorce settlement.

You or your ex can apply to the court for the amount to be increased, decreased, terminated or made payable only for a certain number of years more. For example, if you lose your job or now work part-time your allowance could be increased. If your ex's business is not doing so well, your allowance could be decreased or even terminated. Your allowance, which was awarded on grounds of severe financial hardship, could have a time limit put on it if you were offered a retraining course with a job at the end. If you were awarded an allowance on financial dependency grounds (principle 4),

it cannot be extended beyond three years after divorce.

Your remarriage terminates your periodical allowance automatically. A woman's periodical allowance is usually terminated by the court if she lives with another man even if he is not supporting her, but not all courts take this attitude. Your ex's remarriage can result in your periodical allowance being reduced or terminated if the court thinks his or her commitments have increased. Your periodical allowance should not be reduced if your ex lives with another partner. But if they have children, the court will take these new liabilities into account.

When you die, your periodical allowance comes to an end automatically. But the death of your ex does not mean that your periodical allowance comes to an end automatically. The executors have to apply to the court for it to be terminated. Occasionally the court will then order payment at a reduced rate or set a time limit on the allowance, rather than terminate it.

Any variation the court awards can be backdated to the date of the application, or to the date when the circumstances changed, as long as there was a good reason for the delay in applying for the variation.

Another variation the court can be asked to make is to substitute a lump sum (payable by instalments,

231

perhaps) for a periodical allowance. You and your should weigh up the advantages and disadvantages carefully, because once the substitution order is made it cannot be reversed.

Aliment for children

In exceptional cases (see above) the courts may still award aliment and can vary the amount awarded subsequently. Apart from these cases, if aliment is payable under a court order which was made in proceedings commenced, or a written agreement entered into, before April 1993, the courts retain power to vary the amount. A variation of aliment can be applied for if the circumstances of the child or the paying parent change. The amount of aliment is not reduced merely because the paying parent, or the parent looking after the children, remarries or cohabits. Aliment ceases automatically when either the paying parent or the child dies.

Enforcing maintenance

Legal enforcement methods are called diligence. You do not have to go back to the court, but you will need a solicitor's help. The legal aid certificate for your divorce covers the cost of diligence for up to 12 months later. After a year, or if you are applying for your ex to be imprisoned for failure to pay, you will have to apply for legal aid or legal advice and assistance.

Where your ex is employed, the best diligence to use is a current maintenance arrestment. You (or your solicitor) send a copy of the court order to your ex and if, not less than four weeks later, three or more instalments are in arrears, a current maintenance arrestment can be served by a sheriff officer on your ex's employer. The employer thereafter automatically deducts every payday the maintenance due to you for the period since the last payday and sends it to you or your solicitor. A current maintenance arrestment does not enforce arrears, but you can use an earnings arrestment or another diligence at the same time to recover the arrears.

The following diligences enforce arrears only, although the threat of repeating them may make your ex-spouse keep up regular payments in future.

- Earnings arrestment: a sheriff officer serves a notice on your ex's employer, who deducts every pay-day an amount which varies with the earnings payable then. The deductions are sent to you or your solicitor and stop when the arrears are paid off.
- Arrestment of a bank or building society account: a sheriff officer serves a notice which freezes the

money in your ex's account. You then have to apply to the court for an order requiring the bank or building society to pay you, unless your ex agrees to release the money.

- Attachment and sale of goods: a sheriff officer goes to your ex's home or business premises and makes a list of his or her goods and their value. The court can then order these 'attached' goods to be auctioned to pay the arrears.

- Imprisonment: if the court is satisfied that your ex-'s failure to pay was wilful, he or she can be imprisoned for up to six weeks. Imprisonment is available only for failure to pay aliment; you cannot use it to enforce your periodical allowance.

Effect of divorce on your inheritance rights

After divorce, you have no rights to your ex's estate if he or she dies without a will or leaves you nothing. The Inheritance (Provision for Family and Dependants) Act 1975 does not apply to Scotland.

Legacies or other provisions for you in your ex's will are not cancelled by divorce after the date of the will. Generally speaking, you are entitled to take them unless the will makes it clear that you are not. Your ex's will is not cancelled by his or her subsequent remarriage. If you sign a separation agreement setting out the arrangements for dividing your matrimonial assets, it normally includes a clause giving up your automatic rights of inheritance upon your ex's estate, although the usual provisions contained within the Separation Agreement do not over-rule the terms of an existing Will. You should always remember to review the terms of your Will in the event of separation.

After divorce, you and your ex-should review any existing will. You will probably want to cancel any bequest to your ex-, but other changes may also be desirable. Most married couples who own their home together have in the title deeds that the property will go to the survivor when one of them dies. This is another thing that ought to be changed on or before divorce. A solicitor's help will be needed to change the title deeds.

CHAPTER 10 COHABITING COUPLES

In May 2006, the Scottish Parliament introduced limited rights for Scottish cohabitants.

 For more information see *Which? Essential Guide Wills and Probate* and *Which? Essential Guide Giving and Inheriting*

COHABITANTS' RIGHTS

The Family Law (Scotland) Act 2006, which came into force on 4 May 2006, brought in significant, although limited, rights for unmarried cohabitants for the first time in the United Kingdom. Former cohabitants in Scotland are now, in some circumstances, able to make financial claims against a former partner in a way that is almost akin to seeking financial provision on divorce, or claim certain succession rights on the estate of a former partner following their death where they have left no Will.

The 2006 Act sets out certain broad principles to be applied in the event that a cohabiting couple split or one of them dies without leaving a Will. However, at the time of writing, there is little guidance on how the court will apply these principles. Some applications are now being made to the courts but as yet none have been decided.

The new rights afforded in terms of the 2006 Act apply only to those who ceased cohabitation by reason of separation or death after 4 May 2006 when the legislation came into force.

Definition of Cohabitation

To make a claim, it first needs to be shown that the couple concerned would be regarded as "cohabitants" for the purposes of the Act. A cohabitant is defined as a person who is or was living together with another person as if they were husband and wife or civil partners. In other words, the Act covers male-female and same-sex couples. There is no minimum period of cohabitation. However, the Act also goes on to provide that in determining whether a person is a cohabitant, the courts will have regard to the length and nature of cohabitation, the extent to which the cohabitant is financially dependent on the other and whether the cohabitants have a child of whom they are the parents. It seems possible therefore that a couple who are living together as husband and wife/CPs could be deemed not to have been cohabitants if, for example, they had not been living together for long or their finances remained completely independent.

Financial Provision on Relationship Breakdown

Assuming that you are able to show that you were cohabitants for the purpose of the Act, a number of claims for financial provision can now be made following the breakdown of a relationship (by reason other than death).

1 Right to a share in certain household goods.
There is a presumption that each of you has a right to an equal share in household goods acquired during the period of cohabitation. This would not apply for any household goods acquired by either of you by way of gift or inheritance and does not

include money, cars, caravans, road vehicles, securities or domestic animals. Household goods would be regarded to be any other goods kept or used for joint domestic purpose in any residence in which the cohabitants live or have lived together.

2 Right to a share in certain money and property

Unless there was any agreement to the contrary, for example in terms of a Cohabitation Agreement, a former cohabitant can claim an equal share of any money or property deriving from any allowance made by either of the cohabitants for the joint household expenses or for similar purposes and any property acquired out of such money. "Property" specifically excludes any sole or main residence but could include cars, other motor vehicles, policies etc providing those items were purchased using household allowance or money from a joint account.

3 A claim for payment of a capital sum

A former cohabitant can claim for payment of a capital sum, to be paid by way of a lump sum or in instalments, for their own benefit and/or for a further amount to reflect the additional burden they have of caring for a child of the parties or a child accepted as being a child of the family. Where a claim is being made in respect of a child, that would be most likely to have

to relate to the capital cost of obtaining suitable accommodation for the person making the application and the child to reside in. Maintenance payments for any child would still be dealt with by the Child Support Agency.

A former cohabitant making a claim for payment of a capital sum would have to show that the former partner had derived an economic advantage from the contributions (financial or non financial) that they the claimant had made, and that they the claimant had suffered an economic disadvantage in the interests of either the former partner or of any children of the relationship. They would also then need to show an imbalance in any respective advantages and disadvantages suffered. In looking at whether an economic advantage had been gained or an economic disadvantage suffered, the court would look at gains and losses in respect of capital, income and earning capacity.

Your partner has died without leaving a Will

A claim by a former cohabitant can only be made against the former

 Any claim following on from the breakdown of a relationship must be made to the court within one year of the date of the couple's separation.

partner's estate upon death if the deceased partner died without leaving a Will. A claim can only be made if at the time of death, the deceased was domiciled in Scotland and cohabiting. Any application must be made to the court by the surviving cohabitant within six months of the date of death. The court will consider various factors including the extent and nature of the deceased's estate and any other claims on that estate. Such a claim will not affect an existing spouse's claims against the estate but could act potentially to prejudice any claim by the children of the deceased.

If the financial provisions in the 2006 Act do not apply to you

There are a number of reasons that the rights afforded by the 2006 Act may not be available to you.

Some examples:-

- You may have ceased cohabitation or your partner may have died before 4 May 2006.
- You may wish to apply for a capital sum but cannot show an economic imbalance in respect of the contributions made by you and your partner.
- You may not have made an application to the court timeously, ie, within twelve months of the end of your relationship, or six months after the date of your partner's death.

- You may have entered into a Cohabitation Agreement waiving your right to make such claims.

In circumstances such as these, if you have not entered into a Cohabitation Agreement regulating what is to happen regarding finances in the event of your separation, all that you can rely upon is joint property law or the law of unjustified enrichment.

In terms of the law of joint property, if there is a house which has been purchased in the joint names of yourself and your partner, or a joint bank account, you will each be entitled to a half share of any equity in the property or a half share of the funds held in the account. This may or may not produce what you would consider to be an equitable result.

If you have made financial contributions towards a heritable property which is owned in your former partner's sole name, or title has been taken in proportions that are not reflective of your respective financial contributions, your only possible right of claim may be to rely upon the law of unjustified enrichment. The law of unjustified enrichment is however complicated and the results highly uncertain. The cost of legal fees in making an application under the law of unjustified enrichment are likely to be extremely high with little guarantee of success.

Northern Ireland

To a large extent, divorce in Northern Ireland mirrors that of England and Wales. The most important difference are highlighted in this section.

CHAPTER 4 – MEDIATION AND COLLABORATIVE LAW

There is a Collaborative Law website in operation: news@afriendlydivorce.co.uk.

CHAPTER 5 – DIVORCE AND CHILDREN

Until 4 November 1996 Northern Ireland did not have any legislation in place equivalent to the Children's Act 1989. However, the 1995 order brings legislation relating to children in line with the rest of the UK and creates a new concept of 'parental responsibility'. Where parents are divorcing and there are children of the marriage, the courts in Northern Ireland will no longer make custody or access orders but will make what are termed 'article 8' orders, most important of which are residence and contact orders.

CHAPTER 7 – EMERGENCY MEASURES

In Northern Ireland a spouse or a cohabitant can apply under the Family Homes and Domestic Violence (Northern Ireland) Order 1998 to a court for protection. The protections are the same as the law in England and Wales though there are some local variations in procedure.

CHAPTER 8 – GETTING A DIVORCE / DISSOLUTION

Divorce proceedings cannot be brought within the first two years of marriage.

The 'special procedure' for undefended divorces does not apply to Northern Ireland. The Matrimonial Causes (Northern Ireland) Order 1978 does provide that the Court can dispense with oral testimony where there are special reasons to do so. The petitioner has to apply to the Court for leave to proceed on this basis and such leave is only be granted in exceptional circumstances.

Petitioners must appear in person before a judge and formally prove the ground upon which the petition

Jurisdiction
One or both of you needs to be habitually resident or domiciled in Northern Ireland.

is based, whether in the county court or the High Court. The judge hears the petitioner's evidence in private (known as 'in chambers'), and most undefended divorce hearings are relatively brief (about ten minutes).

WHICH COURT?

In Northern Ireland divorces can be brought in either a county court or the High Court. There is at least one county court for each of the six counties in Northern Ireland, including Recorder's Courts in Londonderry and Belfast. Whether the divorce petition is to be heard in a county court or the High Court is a decision for the petitioner's solicitor. By and large, for petitions that are likely to be defended or in which there are

Financial orders

A revised procedure has now been put into place which applies to all applications from 1 May 2006 onwards and can be found in the Ancillary Relief Guidance Notes for Applications in the High Court at www.courtsni.gov.uk.

sizeable assets to be taken into account, the High Court is considered the more appropriate venue. If a divorce which is issued in the County Court becomes defended then it must be transferred to the High Court (see Chapter 9).

Fees

Stamp duty payable on a divorce petition is £155 in a county court and £170 in the High Court. To set the divorce down for Hearing in a county court there is a fee of £82 and £98 in the High Court. The application for a Decree Absolute in either Court costs £23.

Family Mediation NI: 028 9024 3265
Relate NI: 0870 2426091 www.relateni.org
Law Society of Northern Ireland: 028 9024 1614 www.lawsoc-ni.org

Appendices

APPENDIX A: APPLYING THE CHILD SUPPORT AGENCY FORMULA

Step 1 Work out the net income of the non-resident parent (NRP)

Weekly income (including regular overtime and tax credits) less:
- Income tax
- National Insurance
- Pension contributions

Ignore:
- Child benefit
- Housing benefit
- Council tax benefit
- Student loans and grants
- Income from lodgers (unless it is a significant source of income)
- Non-contributory benefits for people with disabilities (such as disability living allowance and attendance allowance)

> The CSA is able to calculate maintenance on the net income of the NRP only up to £2,000 a week. If the income is higher than this, you may be able to get a top up order from the court.

Step 2 Decide whether it would be appropriate to apply any variation

For detailed information see: CSA leaflet CSL108 Child support variations: Help for exceptional circumstances. You can get a reduction if:
- You have costs relating to keeping in contact with a child for whom you are paying maintenance.
- You have extra expenses because a child who lives with you has a disability or a long-term illness.
- You are still paying off a debt that you took on for the family before you separated.
- You are paying boarding school fees for a child for whom you are paying maintenance.
- You are paying a mortgage, loan or insurance on the former home, you no longer have an interest in it and your (former) spouse/partner and the children still live there.

If these costs amount to £10 or less and your net income is below £200, or £15 or less where your net income is £200 or more, then you will not get a reduction (though this restriction does not apply to expenses for a sick child or a child with a disability).

You will also not be able to use a variation to reduce the maintenance to less than £5 per week or, at the other end of the scale, if your net weekly income is more than £2,000 and would still be over that amount once the variation was deducted.

Step 3   Apply the appropriate rate: basic, reduced, flat or nil.

Basic rate

Number of children	% of NRP net income
1	15%
2	20%
3 or more	25%

Maintenance payments
Note that maintenance is worked out on a weekly basis to the nearest whole pound. Amounts of 50p and over are rounded up

If the NRP has other children for whom he receives child benefit (these are known as 'relevant children', such as children from a second marriage), the rate of maintenance is calculated by applying the percentages above to the net income after first deducting a similar percentage for the relevant child(ren) (see box below).

Reduced rate

If a NRP's net weekly income is more than £100 but less than £200 you take:
• A flat rate of £5 per week, plus
• A percentage of the net weekly income over £100.
The percentages used are shown in the Reduced Rate table.

Reduced rate %		Qualifying children		
		1	2	3
Relevant	0	25%	35%	45%
other	1	20.5%	29%	37.5%
children	2	19%	27%	35%
	3	17.5%	25%	32.5%

Step 3 (continued)

Flat rate

Maintenance is paid at a 'flat rate' of £5 per week if the NRP's net weekly income is £100 or less, or if he or she is in receipt of any of the following:

- income support
- jobseeker's allowance
- retirement pension
- incapacity benefit
- widow's benefits
- war pension
- severe disablement allowance
- invalid care allowance
- industrial injuries disablement benefit
- contribution-based jobseeker's allowance

Nil rate

for NRPs with an income of less than £5 per week or who are:

- students or young people in full-time education
- prisoners
- 16- or 17-year-olds on income support/income-based jobseekers' allowance
- people in residential care or nursing homes receiving help with fees.

Step 4 Make any appropriate deductions for shared care

Shared care – basic and reduced rate

If you share the care of the child(ren) so that from time to time they stay overnight with the NRP, this will decrease the amount of maintenance payable. You have to look at the number of nights that the children have spent with the NRP over the last 12 months or, if the break-up is new, the projected number of nights in the next year. The reductions are:

Number of nights	Subtract
52 to 103	one-seventh
104 to 155	two-sevenths
156 to 174	three-sevenths
175 or more	one-half

If there is more than one child and you have different amounts of staying time for the different children, calculate the reduction by adding the appropriate fraction for each child, and dividing the total by the number of children.

If the NRP looks after a child for 175 nights or more each year, you have to make an additional reduction in the maintenance of £7 for each child.

The lowest limit to which the maintenance can be decreased is £5 per week. (If there are children with different PWCs, the £5 minimum would be divided as described below.)

Shared care – flat rate
If the child(ren) spend(s) at least 52 nights a year with the NRP, who would otherwise be paying at the flat rate, then the maintenance reduces to nil.

Children with different PWCs – apportionment
If a NRP has children who have different PWCs the amount of child support payable will be apportioned between the different PWCs. The amount payable will be divided by the number of children and shared depending on how many children each parent with care has.

For more information go to:
www.cas.gov.uk

APPENDIX B: YOUR RIGHTS IF YOU SHARE A RENTED HOME

Private tenancy or Housing Association tenancy since 15.1.1989 in one person's name

↓

Tenant can give other person notice to quit. There is no protection for the non-tenant. If the tenant leaves, you can ask landlord to assign the tenancy but you can't compel him to do so

---

Private tenancy or Housing Association tenancy since 15.1.1989 in joint names.

| Assured tenancy or statutory periodic tenancy. | Regulated or protected tenancy. |

↓ ↓

In a periodic tenancy either of you can give notice to quit, ending it. You can stop your partner doing it (see box). You must get a new tenancy granted to you. In a fixed tenancy you need the landlord's consent to end it or stay liable.

If one of you leaves the other can stay, and, by giving notice, prevent the other one from returning.

Council tenancy or Housing Association tenancy before 15.1.1989 in one person's name.

↓

Tenant can give other person notice to quit. The non-tenant has no rights to stay. Tenant can assign the tenancy by 'deed'. If tenant leaves, the tenancy ends, but you can ask council to grant tenancy to person who stays if s/he shows housing need.

Council tenancy or Housing Association tenancy before 15.1.1989 in joint names.

↓

You must decide who will stay, unless you both decide to leave. Either can give notice to quit which will end the tenancy. You can stop your partner doing this (see box). You must get a new tenancy granted to you.

Under Schedule 7 of the Family Law Act 1996 you can ask the court to transfer the tenancy to one of you. The court will not be able to do this if the tenancy has been ended by one tenant giving notice to quit. If you need to you can get a court order to prevent the notice being given. If you have children you can also apply for a transfer of the tenancy under Sch. 1 of the Children Act 1989.

Appendices

Useful addresses

Alcoholics Anonymous
National helpline: 0845 769 7555
www.alcoholics-anonymous.org.uk

Asian Family Counselling Service
Tel/Fax: 020 8571 3933/020 8813 9714
www.asianfamilycounselling.org.uk

Association for Shared Parenting
Tel 01789 751157
Fax: 01789 751081.
www.sharedparenting.org.uk

Both Parents Forever
Tel: (01689) 854343
www.bvsc.co.uk/chd/bothparentsforever.htm
(Help/advice to parents/grandparents
involved in separation, divorce, care
proceedings or child abduction.

British Association of Lawyer Mediators
Tel: 7000 766 422
www.lawwise.co.uk/balm.html

Childline
Helpline: (0800) 1111
www.childline.org.uk

Comprehensive Accredited Lawyer Mediators
Caroline Graham MacLeod &MacCallum
Tel: 01463 239393
www.macandmac.co.uk

Council of Mortgage Lenders
Information line: 020 7438 8956
www.cml.org.uk

Dawn (South Yorkshire Surviving
Separation and Divorce
01709 309130
www.dawnproject.org.uk

Department for Work and Pensions (DWP)
www.dwp.gov.uk
For general queries contact your local office

Principal Registry Of the Family Division
Tel: 020 7947 6000

www.divorceaid.co.uk

Families Need Fathers
Helpline: 0870 7607 496
www.fnf.org.uk

Family Law Association of Scotland
www.fla-scotland.co.uk

Family Mediation Scotland
Tel: 0845 119 2020
www.familymediationscotland.org.uk

Family Welfare Assocation
Tel: 020 7254 6251
www.fwa.org.uk

Gingerbread
Tel: 020 7403 9500
Advice line: 0800 018 4318
(weekdays 10am-12pm/1pm-3pm)
www.gingerbread.org.uk
This is a support organisation which
publishes advice and information leaflets
and offers support to lone parents and
their families, with around 200 groups
in England and Wales.

Jewish Marriage Council
Counselling line: 020 8203 6311
www.jmc-uk.org

Law Society of Scotland
Tel: 0845 1130018
www.lawscot.org.uk

London Lesbian and Gay Switchboard
Tel: 020 7837 7324 (24 hours)
www.llgs.org.uk

National Children's Bureau
Tel: 020 7843 6000
www.ncb.org.uk

National Debtline
Tel: 0808 808 4000
www.nationaldebtline.co.uk

National Family Mediation (NFM)
Tel: 01392 271610
www.nfm.org.uk

National Housing Federation
Tel: 020 7067 1010
www.housing.org.uk

Northern Ireland Housing Executive
Tel: 028 9024 0588
www.nihe.gov.uk

Northern Ireland Legal Services Commission
Tel: 028 9040 8888
www.nilsc.org.uk

Northern Ireland Women's Aid Federation
Helpline: 0800 917 1414 (24 hours)

One Parent Families
Tel: 020 7428 5400
Helpline: 0800 018 5026
(weekdays 9am–5pm)
www.oneparentfamilies.org.uk

One Parent Families Scotland
Tel: 0131 556 3899
www.opfs.org.uk

Relate Scotland
Tel: 0845 119 6088
Email: enquiries@couplecounselling.org
www.couplecounselling.org

Scottish Marriage Care
Tel: 0141 222 2166
www.scottishmarriagecare.org

Scottish Women's Aid
Helpline: 0800 027 1234
www.scottishwomensaid.co.uk

Glossary

Annuity Money investment designed to produce regular fixed amounts of income, either for a fixed period or until death.

Application A document giving broad details of the order sought from the court. All applications within divorce proceedings begin by filing a notice of application.

Care and attention A term used to describe an uplift (increase) in a solicitor's legal bill, which some solicitors apply if a case has been complex or has had to be dealt with especially quickly.

In chambers When the district judge or judge considers an application in private rather than in open court; the proceedings tend to be less formal than normal court hearings and members of the public are not admitted.

Charge (on property) Security entitling the holder of the charge to be paid out of the proceeds of sale when the house (or other property) is eventually sold.

Chattels An old-fashioned legal term used for personal effects, usually of a house, like furniture, paintings, jewellery and ornaments.

Community Legal Service (CLS) The body that oversees the granting of public funding for legal cases. Formerly the Legal Aid Board.

Conditional order A decree nisi in a cp divorce.

Conflict of interest(s) Where a solicitor cannot act for a potential client because he or she would be unable to discharge his or her duty to the client, owing to a pre-existing professional relationship to another client or a duty owed to another.

Disclosure Full information about all matters relevant to any financial application; each spouse has a duty to give full and frank disclosure which, if they fail to abide by, may render a later court order invalid.

Discovery Procedure by which each party supplies to the other a list of documents relevant to an application and permits the other to inspect them.

Dissolution order A final decree in a cp divorce.

District judge Judicial officer appointed by the Lord Chancellor; responsible for dealing with most applications to a divorce court (used to be called a registrar).

Divorce court Any county court designated by the Lord Chancellor as a court where divorce proceedings can be heard; the Divorce Registry in London serves as a divorce court. Divorce county courts not designated as Family Hearing Centres (FHCs; q.v.) can deal only with the administrative process of divorces; any contested applications will be referred to an FHC.

Domicile Legal concept, not necessarily related to residence: domicile of origin is normally determined by the place where a person was born and is retained, unless a new domicile – a domicile of choice – is adopted by a conscious decision to take up permanent residence in, and actually move to, another country.

Equity (of a property) The net value of house or flat after mortgage debts are discharged and expenses of sale met exhibit Document referred to in, sworn with, and attached to an affidavit; usually identified by initials and number.

Ex parte An old term for an application made directly to the court without prior notification to the party or parties.

Family Hearing Centre A county court with the power to deal with the administrative process of divorce and any contested applications under the Children Act, or for financial relief.

Filing Leaving documents – petition and accompanying documents, affidavits, notices of application, for example – with the court office for sealing, and subsequent service.

Hearsay evidence A fact reported to a witness, as opposed to being known by the witness; second-hand knowledge; hearsay evidence can be accepted by a court in family proceedings.

Injunction Order by the court telling someone what he or she must do or must refrain from doing; the penalty for disobedience can be imprisonment.

Intestacy Dying without a valid will.

Maintenance Application Form and Maintenance Enquiry Form Standard forms sent out by the Child Support Agency to parents with care and absent parents respectively, asking them about their means and circumstances.

Matrimonial home rights Rights of occupation of a family home (or a home intended to be occupied as a family home) which last until decree absolute.

Mediation An alternative form of dispute resolution over issues arising in the wake of separation or divorce. Comprehensive (or 'all issues') mediation covers problems over both children and finances; other mediation (or conciliation: the terms are sometimes used interchangeably) services may deal with child-related disputes alone. Mediation may be offered by lawyer mediators or family mediators, alone or both together.

Minutes of order Draft terms of agreement placed before the court with a request that a consent order be made in those terms.

Mortgagee The building society, bank or other corporate lender, or individual lending money on the security of a house or flat.

Mortgagor The person who borrows money on mortgage, usually to enable him or her to buy a house or flat.

Nominal order An order for a nominal amount of maintenance (for example, 5p a year) made if, at the time an order for maintenance was made, payment could not be made or was not needed. This is done so that, if circumstances change, there is an order on the court's file which can be reviewed and increased.

Non-molestation order Order to prohibit one person from assaulting, harassing or interfering with another.

Notice of application Form on which applications to the court are made, starting with the words 'Take notice that ...' and containing details of what is applied for.

Ouster Order excluding one spouse from the matrimonial home (or from part of it).

Penal notice A warning endorsed on a court order, notifying the recipient that

he or she is liable to committal to prison for breach of the order.

Pending suit While the divorce is still continuing (i.e. before decree absolute).

Pleadings Formal statements or documents containing a summary of the issues in a case.

Public funding Another term for 'legal aid': state financial assistance with the cost of legal proceedings. Note: generally requires repayment by the 'statutory charge'.

Questionnaire List of questions delivered by one spouse to the other requiring further information and/or documentation about finances, in accordance with that person's duty of disclosure.

Recovered or preserved Gained or retained (money or property) in the course of legal proceedings.

Relevant child Child of the family under 16 years of age at the date of the decree nisi, or between 16 and 18 years of age and receiving instruction at an educational establishment, or undergoing training for a trade, profession or vocation (or up to any age, if disabled and dependent).

Reply Document filed by the petitioner in response to an answer and/or a cross-petition from the respondent, containing the petitioner's defence.

Reserved costs When decision on amount of costs to be awarded is deferred until later hearing.

Sealing by the court The court's stamping of a document when it is filed at the court office or of an order or decree when it is issued.

Secured provision When some income-producing asset of the payer is put under the control of trustees and, if necessary, the income diverted to the payee to provide the maintenance.

SERPS The earnings part of state retirement pension, based on National Insurance contributions paid by an employee on earnings between the lower and upper earnings limits.

Service The method by which the petition, notices of application, orders and decrees are supplied to the parties concerned; certain documents need to be served personally, others are served through the post, some by or on behalf of the person issuing them and some by the court.

Statutory charge The amount payable by a publicly funded person out of any property or cash that was recovered or preserved in the proceedings, where contributions to the Legal Services Commission are not sufficient to meet the legal costs of the case.

Summons Demand issued by a court for a person against whom a claim or complaint has been made to appear at the court at a specified time

undefended divorce Where the dissolution of the marriage and how it is to be achieved are not disputed (even if there is dispute about ancillary matters such as the children or finances).

Undertaking Promise to the court to do or not do something which is outside the court's powers to order but is incorporated within a court order so that it is enforceable; the court has no power of its own to vary an undertaking.

Unfunded scheme A pension scheme where the employee has a right or expectation to a pension benefit secured only by an undertaking from the employer, for example in a contract of employment; no advance financial provision is made via trust fund or other insurance contract.

Without prejudice Phrase used to prevent communications in the negotiation process being made known to the court at the final hearing if those negotiations fail to produce agreement; however, offers and responses to them can be disclosed to the court in evidence over costs.

Index

Which? Books

Which? Books provide impartial, expert advice on everyday matters from finance to law, property to major life events. We also publish the country's most trusted restaurant guide, *The Which? Good Food Guide.* To find out more about Which? Books, log on to www.which.co.uk or call 01903 828557.

Other books in this series

Which? Essential Guides
Buying Property Abroad

Jeremy Davies
ISBN: 978-1844-900-244

A complete guide to the legal, financial and practical aspects of buying property abroad. This book provides down-to-earth advice on how the buying process differs from the UK, and how to negotiate contracts, commission surveys, and employ lawyers and architects. Practical tips on currency deals and taxes – and how to command the best rent – all ensure you can buy abroad with total peace of mind.

Which? Essential Guides
Buy, Sell and Move House

Kate Faulkner
ISBN: 978-1844-900-305

A complete, no-nonsense guide to negotiating the property maze and making your move as painless as possible. From dealing with estate agents to chasing solicitors, working out the true cost of your move to understanding Home Information Packs, this guide tells you how to keep things on track and avoid painful sticking points.

❝Which? tackles the issues that really matter to consumers and gives you the advice and active support you need to buy the right products.❞